Cryptocurrencies

An Essential Beginner's Guide to Blockchain Technology, Cryptocurrency Investing, Mastering Bitcoin Basics Including Mining, Ethereum Smart Contracts, Trading and Some Info on Programming

Contents

CRYPTOCURRENCIES 3

PART 1: BLOCKCHAIN 1

SECTION 1: MONEY AS WE NOW KNOW IT: THE PAST & PRESENT . 2

THE HISTORY OF MONEY 3

THE ORIGINS OF MONEY AND BANKING 6

    Functions Of Money 6

FACTORS THAT LED TO THE DEVELOPMENT OF MONEY 7

    Money in Its Primitive Form 9

THE INVENTION OF COINS AND BANKING 10

HOW MONEY EXCHANGES AND CREDIT TRANSFER DEVELOPED 12

HOW CURRENCY CENTRALIZATION AND MONOPOLY OVER MONEY-MINTING
STARTED 15

    Early Forms of Counterfeit Currency Checks 16

THE INTRODUCTION OF PAPER MONEY 18

MONEY IN THE PRESENT: PLASTIC MONEY 18

SECTION 2: UNDERSTANDING THE BLOCKCHAIN TECHNOLOGY 20

BLOCKCHAIN 101: A SUCCINCT GUIDE 21

WHAT IS THE BLOCKCHAIN TECHNOLOGY? 22

HISTORY OF THE BLOCKCHAIN 27

A CHRONOLOGICAL DEVELOPMENT OF BLOCKCHAIN RELATED TECHNOLOGIES
.... 30

BENEFITS OF THE BLOCKCHAIN TECHNOLOGY 34

DISADVANTAGES OF USING BLOCKCHAIN TECHNOLOGY 39

SECTION 3: ETHEREUM GUIDE FOR BEGINNERS **47**

UNDERSTANDING ETHEREUM 47

HOW ETHEREUM DEVELOPED...49

HOW ETHEREUM WORKS..51

HOW SMART CONTRACTS WORK...52

THE APPLICATION POSSIBILITIES FOR SMART CONTRACTS..............................57

MINING: HOW MINING WORKS..61

SECTION 4: A TECHNICAL GUIDE TO GETTING STARTED ON
BLOCKCHAIN...**64**

GETTING STARTED ON BLOCKCHAIN: IMPLEMENTING BLOCKCHAIN INTO
BUSINESS OPERATIONS 65

BLOCKCHAIN-BASED APPLICATIONS YOU CAN INTEGRATE INTO YOUR
BUSINESS 68

SMART CONTRACT AND ETHEREUM WEB DEVELOPMENT: A PRACTICAL
GETTING-STARTED GUIDE 71

SECTION 5: THE FUTURE OF MONEY: A CRYPTOCURRENCIES ET
AL GUIDE FOR BEGINNERS...**84**

UNDERSTANDING CRYPTOCURRENCIES AND THEIR EMERGENCE......................85

HOW CRYPTOCURRENCIES WORK 88

BITCOIN LIFECYCLE: HOW CRYPTOCURRENCY TRANSACTIONS WORK...........91

HOW TO INVEST IN BLOCKCHAIN AND CRYPTOCURRENCIES 93

CONCLUSION **95**

PART 2: BITCOIN..**96**

INTRODUCTION **97**

UNDERSTANDING CRYPTOCURRENCY: AN INTRODUCTION TO
CRYPTOCURRENCY & THE SIMPLEST EXPLANATION OF BITCOIN
AND CRYPTOCURRENCY THAT YOU WILL EVER READ **99**

AN INTRODUCTION TO CRYPTOCURRENCY...99

WHAT IS CRYPTOCURRENCY? 99

HOW DOES BITCOIN, AND BY EXTENSION, MOST CRYPTOCURRENCIES WORK?
....100

THE SIMPLEST EXPLANATION FOR BITCOIN AND CRYPTOCURRENCY THAT YOU WILL EVER READ 101

DEFINITION OF TERMS 106

BLOCKCHAIN TECHNOLOGY 112

COMPARISON BETWEEN DIGITAL CURRENCY & FIAT CURRENCY 114

INVESTING IN BITCOIN 116

GETTING STARTED 117

STEPS TO INVESTING IN BITCOIN 119

Step 1: Creating A Bitcoin Wallet 119

Long Term Storage Of Bitcoin 125

Step 2: Connect Your Wallet To Your Bank Account 131

Step 3: Using Funds In Your Bank Account To Buy Bitcoin 134

Step 4: Trading With Bitcoin 137

Getting Started With CFDS 142

Bitcoin Day Trading 146

Bitcoin Arbitrage Trading 148

Bitcoin Margin Trading 150

Bitcoin Binary Trading 152

Tips For Successful Binary Trading 153

BITCOIN MINING 155

How To Mine Bitcoins 156

Bitcoin Cloud Mining 159

How Cloud Mining Works 160

TIPS FOR INVESTING IN BITCOIN 162

THE FUTURE OF BITCOIN 165

CONCLUSION 167

PART 3: ETHEREUM 168

INTRODUCTION 169

CHAPTER 1: ETHEREUM: A COMPREHENSIVE BACKGROUND 171

WHAT IS ETHEREUM? 171

BLOCKCHAIN TECHNOLOGY 171

USES OF ETHEREUM 176

SMART CONTRACTS 186

THE ETHER 190

ETHEREUM VIRTUAL MACHINE (EVM) 192

CHAPTER 2: INVESTING IN ETHEREUM 194

THE ETHER WALLET 203

BUYING ETHEREUM 209

DAY TRADING ETHEREUM 216

CHAPTER 3: ETHEREUM MINING 223

WHAT'S ETHEREUM MINING? 224

THE IMPORTANCE OF ETHEREUM MINING 228

THE ETHEREUM MINING PROCEDURE 232

ETHEREUM CLOUD MINING 236

ETHEREUM MINING PROFITABILITY CALCULATOR 238

CHAPTER 4: THE FUTURE OF ETHEREUM 241

CONCLUSION 245

Part 1: Blockchain

An Essential Beginner's Guide to Understanding Blockchain Technology, Cryptocurrencies, Bitcoin and the Future of Money

Section 1: Money as We Now Know It: The Past & Present

Before we can discuss the disruptive role cryptocurrencies play in the future of money, we have to look at the history of money because it is in this history that we learn why currencies such as bitcoins, altcoins, Litecoins, and other cryptocurrencies that use the blockchain technology came into being.

Understanding how money came into being and how we used it in the past shall help us understand how and why currencies that use the blockchain technology are revolutionizing money and how we use it.

The History of Money

Money as we know it today is not one thing, per se. Today, money is a series of interconnected technologies that have developed over time starting from barter trade, beads, gold, coins, and then paper money.

In relation to what experts have to say about our historical use of money, two main ideas spring out. The first one is that, as indicated earlier, the need for currency, i.e. money, came from problems with the reliability of barter trade in that by bartering, it was impossible to tell if what you bartered for was worth what you gave in return. The other theorem is that governments are responsible for creating money as a way to settle debt. Both ideas have merit. Here is why.

If you look at the barter trade idea and trace it back to its roots (which is a long time ago), the story you will reveal is one where swapping one good for the other was the order of the day. For instance, if John Doe was a pot maker and at the approach of winter, he needed blankets, he would go to Jane Smith, a weaver and if she needed pots, they would barter.

As you can imagine, this sort of trading had an element of inequality in that there was no pre-agreed upon rate at which to barter. A large pot could trade for 2, 5, 10, or even 20 blankets depending on the temperament and the desperateness of the traders. This meant that this form of trade was open to manipulation because in an instance where you had pots, desperately wanted blankets, but could not find someone to trade with at a favorable rate, you would end up bartering your pots for less than their worth.

As is visible, such inequality and difficult of trade precipitated the introduction of standards, which is how, as the story goes, man decided to come up with a convenient way to trade by creating a standard using valuable things such as beads, shells, and coins. This standardization meant that specific items would have a trade standard. For instance, a pig, chicken, or even X amount of pots and blankets would translate into a specific amount of the valuable thing. For instance, a pig would trade for X amounts of beads.

The second theory, the one about governments forming money as a way to cushion against debt, also has some merit in that many anthropologists agree that the earliest forms of money as we now know it emerged in Mesopotamia around 5,000 years ago.

Anthropologists postulate that the bureaucrats running the royal palace created the earliest units of money as a way to measure wages, settle debts between landowners and traders, and calculate fines and taxes. In this bureaucracy, money took a standardized form as weights of silver. The government of the day took it upon themselves to determine the value of the silver not based on the value of the metal, but based on their own interest. From a broader perspective, this story also has some basing in truth. Here is why:

When you look at our use of money in modern day life, you can see that the regulation of banknotes by governments the world over is very similar to what the Mesopotamian government did thousands of years ago and therefore, this regulation by the Mesopotamian government could very well be the start of centralized currencies.

These two accounts of how money came into being complement each other in that they allow us to see how differently we understand money and the role it has to play in trade and society in general.

In the barter version, money developed spontaneously without any governmental intervention and out of necessity as trade between individuals changed. On the other hand, the anthropological account postulates that a public institution, the government or an arm of it, is responsible for developing money as a way to help the public settle debts owed to each other and to the government in form of trade taxes and land lease.

To understand the history of money in its entirety, we have to dig deeper because this history is one that led to the formation of money and banking as we now know it and without proper understanding of this, we cannot understand how currencies of the future are changing everything we know about money.

The Origins of Money and Banking

Chris Skinner, a leading commentator and strategist on the financial markets, believes that the creation of shared beliefs is what led to the creation of money and banking (at least elements of it) because these beliefs are what bind us together; they allow us to work together and get along.

If you ask a layman, the average person walking in the street, to define money, the answer you get is bound to be a simplistic one: coin and banknotes. This answer, while simplistic, leaves a lot uncovered. For instance, what about credit cards, cheques, and gold; do these not count as forms of money?

The point here is that throughout history, and even today, money has taken many shapes and forms. For instance, as we have discussed above, money has taken the form of things such as beads, amber, eggs, leather, gold, zappozats, and many other forms such as ivory, salt, and even yarns. This makes it very impossible to define money in terms of physical properties. To define money, we have to define it using its various functions.

Functions Of Money

The functions of money are vast. Other than the common uses as a medium of exchange, means of payment, and store of value, money is also a unit of account, a common measure of value, and a standard of deferred payments. From a macro-economic perspective, money is also a liquid asset, a controller of the economy, a framework of the market allocative system in terms of prices, and a causative factor in the economy.

From these defined functions of money, you can see that not all things used as money serve all these functions and that how a particular form of money functions may change drastically over time. In relation to this, Glyn Davies, author of the wildly popular book, *A History of Money From Ancient Times to the Present Day*, and an expert on the history of money, has the following to say:

"What is now the prime or main function of money in a particular community or country may not have been the first or original function in time, while what may well have been a secondary or derived function in one place may have been in some other region the original which gave rise to a related secondary function..."

This is an excerpt from the book.

Davies goes on to conclude that the best definition of money is the following: "Money is anything widely used to make payments and account for debts and credits." That is the best definition of money and the one we shall use as we delve deeper into this discussion.

Factors that Led to the Development of Money

We cannot discuss money without discussing the causative factors that led to the development of it. While our previous discussion on the subject partly illuminated this, we have to throw more light on it.

In his book, Davies implies the following:

"Contrary to popular belief and in clear contrast with the anthropological account of how money came into being, money mainly developed from economic causes."

He says that other than developing from barter, money developed for tribute purposes, to serve as trade and bribe money, and for ceremonial and religious rites. He goes further to state that money also developed from commerce, ostentatious ornamentation, and as a common drudge between economic men.

From this account, one of the things we can derive is that the most important improvements on barter trade happened when those bartering tended to select one or more items in preference to others to a point where the widely selected item gained wide acceptance as the standard of quality and the preferred medium of exchange.

The causative reason for this, i.e. the reason why some items became the preferred items for barter trade, varies. Some of these reasons included items being easier to store, some having higher value and density, easier to port, and some because they were durable and considered valuable. Because those trading widely accepted these commodities, they became desirable, and since they were easier to exchange for others, they became the widely accepted form of money.

Even though the disadvantages of barter trade are part of the catalyst that led to the development of money, this catalyst was economic and from archeological, linguistic, literally, and even tangible evidence of primitive forms of money in many ancient worlds, barter plays a very marginal role in the development and origin of the earliest forms of money.

From this context and from archeological evidence, many societies had in place laws dictating how those engaging in violent crimes would "pay." The word pay comes from the Latin word "pacare," a word whose original meaning is to make peace with, appease, or pacify. From a historical context, this means those caught in crime would pay through a unit of value customarily accepted by all.

This account illuminates the following: that in many societies, there were required means of payment for tax, tribute, bride-money, and blood money, all of which lead to the widespread use of money. This account also illustrates that the use of money did not singularly evolve from the disadvantages or use of barter trade. It developed from deeply rooted customs, the shortcomings of barter trade, and in most parts of the world, it evolved independently.

Money in Its Primitive Form

From historical documentation, the use of primitive forms of money in North America and the Third World is better than that of Europe. This documentation throws light on the probable origins of modern forms of money.

As an example, documented history shows that North America widely used Wampum and the tradition of potlatch for gift exchange. Africa widely used cowrie shells, Asia used whale teeth, cattle, and Manillas, and Yap used disc-shaped stones. In West Africa, Manillas were ornamental metal objects worn as jewelry and used as money even as recent as 1949. In North America, the use of Wampum as money came from its desirability as an ornament and since metals have had ornamental uses throughout history, this could explain their uptake and use as money in many civilizations.

In historical context, whale teeth found use as bride-money in certain Fijian societies (some Fijian societies still use them to date) with their use having the same meaning as engagement rings in today's societies.

The Invention of Coins and Banking

Which of the two, coinage and banking, do you think preceded the other? In a normal instance, it would seem that coins would come before banking. Well, that is not the case, and in reality, the invention of banking came before that of coinage.

The earliest form of banking recorded originated in Mesopotamia where temples and royal palaces provided to those in need safe places to store their grains and other commodities they considered valuable. Later, this society started using the receipts issued for the storage of these valuables not only for transfer to the original depositor, but also for transfer to third parties. This setup flourished so much that privately owned homes in Mesopotamia started offering similar banking operations and before long, the royals started introducing into the code of Hammurabi, laws regulating these banking operations.

Ancient Egyptians also had a similar system. For instance, the Egyptians implemented centralization of harvest: they stored their harvest in state warehouses, something that led to the development of the banking system in that society. From this system, those who had stored grains in the warehouses would require written orders before withdrawing their lot of grains or lots deposited in credit of the king. This became the generally accepted form of payment for debts to tax gatherers, priests and other traders, and long after the introduction of coins, the Egyptian system was very helpful in that it helped reduce the demand for precious metal coins otherwise reserved for major foreign purchases of a military nature.

Shells made in China from copper and bronze are among the earliest forms of countable monies. The Chinese also produced coins from other things such as hoes, knives, spades, and other objects widely accepted as forms of money. In ancient Greek, the Greeks used iron nails as coins and as history has it, Julius Caesar considered the Britons backward for using sword blades as coins.

The quasi-coins of the early days were too easy to counterfeit and since they were of low intrinsic value and made of base metals, they were not convenient for expensive purchases.

The Lydians, residents of Asia Minor, take home the trophy for developing true coinage. They did so by stamping small rounded pieces of precious metals as a sign of their guaranteed purity and value. When their metal fashioning skills improved, they started creating regular forms of these monies and because the weight was also regular, the monies they created become a symbol of value and purity. In relation to the first coins ever minted, historians postulate that this happened between 630-640 BC and later spread from Lydia to Persia and mainland Greece.

Usage of Coin In Ancient Greece

Greece is home to some of man's most relevant historical events. In relation to the development of money, Greece had the silver obol, one of the smaller forms of Greek coins. In ancient Greek, the standards of weights varied depending on location. The system of weight and measures also changed as needed. In relation to this and using the Attic standard of weight and measure, 6 silver obols amounted to one silver drachma.

Like today, in the early days of the development of coins, inflation posed a problem. For instance, in 407 BC after Sparta stormed Athens, took control over the Athenian mines, and released over 20,000 working slaves, Athens faced a grave coin shortage. To rectify this, they issued bronze coins that had a thin plating of silver. Unfortunately, this worsened the shortage and since good coins were valuable, people tended to keep them instead of using them. They opted to use the new ones, which led to increased usage and inflation.

How Money Exchanges and Credit Transfer Developed

As you can see from the above discussion, the exchange of coins in early worlds such as Greece may very well be the earliest form of banking. For example, in Greece, moneychangers would situate their trapezium-shaped tables and themselves around temples and public places. The Greeks called these bankers *trapezitai*, a name derived from the Italian word *banca*, meaning bench or counter, which is where our name for modern banks comes from.

In these early societies, money changing was not the only form of service offered by these 'bankers.' Of the many services offered by these early bankers, key among them was bottomry, a term used to refer to ships lending freight services. The Greek bankers also played a role in the financing of mining and the construction of public buildings.

Like the world famous J.P Morgan, an American financier, Pasion was the most famous and richest of these bankers. He grew his business empire by charging a lucrative fee on lending silver bowls, blankets, clothes, and by owning the largest shield factory in all of Greece.

After the fall of Egypt under the rule of the Greek dynasty, the system of warehouse banking we discussed earlier gained a new level of sophistication. Instead of being scattered warehouses, the ruling dynasty, then the Ptolemies, consolidated the warehouse to form a sophisticated network of grains storage units with what we can only refer to as the "central bank" situated in Alexandria. This "central bank" became home to the main accounts of records for all state granary banks.

The system functioned as a form of giro system where payments happened through transference without the explicit need of money changing hands. Since this was before the invention of double entry booking, this method used a system where the officials in charge recorded the credit transfers by changing the different case endings of all involved names. Credit entries used the possessive, or genitive case, while debit used the dative case.

In the late second and third centuries BC, credit transfer was one of the key services offered in Delos, a barren offshore island whose inhabitants had to be witty to survive the barrenness of their land. To develop their financial and trading activities, they utilized their two greatest assets: the famous temple of Apollo and the island's beautiful harbor. In comparison to Athens, where the early forms of banking was exclusively in the form of cash, Delos had a system that used real credit receipts; clients who had accounts could make payments on simple instructions.

The banks of Rome closely imitated the formatting of the bank of Delos after Delos' main commercial rivals, Carthage and Corinth, fell at the mercies of Rome. However, unlike Delos, the Romans preferred cash transactions with coins. The fall of the Roman Empire also brought with it the fall of banking.

The reinvention of banking happened much later in Europe at the time of the Crusades. More specifically, Italian cities such as Genoa, Rome and Venice, and medieval French fairs found a need for banking services since they had to transfer large sums of money for purposes of trade. This need precipitated the development of payment/financial services such as bills of exchange.

While the Arabs and the Jews may have used such modes of payments as early as 8th and 10th century, definitive evidence of the use of bills of exchange is in 1156 in Genoa when two brothers took a 'loan' of 115 Genoese pounds. The brothers had to repay the bank's agents by paying 460 bezants a month after arriving in Constantinople.

The age of the Crusades was a stimulus to banking because in that age, there was need for the safe transfer of cash for payment to allies and payment for equipment, ransom, and even supplies. Knights of the Temple and Hospitallers started offering banking service such as those provide by Italian cities as discussed earlier.

How Currency Centralization and Monopoly over Money-Minting Started

If you look at today's society and the rules that govern money, you will realize that governments the world over monopolize the printing of coin or paper money and that in many jurisdictions printing money is illegal and punishable by law. Governmental monopoly over the printing of money is not new; it has a long history.

As we have already stated in more than one instance, their ease of use and porting is one of the reasons why civilizations the world over rapidly took up the use of coins. In instances where the value of the coin did not depend on its weight, traders did not find the need to weigh the coins; they simply accepted them at their nominal value. However, in everyday transactions, counting the coins was easier, quicker, and far more convenient, something monarchs started profiting from at the start of the middle ages.

In his book, Glyn Davies has the following to say about this:

"Since royally authenticated coinage was the most convenient mode of payment, most coins had a substantial premium over their metallic value; in most instances, this value was more than high enough to cover the cost of minting the coins. Kings turned this premium into profit, which is why in the early days, there were wholesale recalls of coinage starting with 6 times yearly until it became 2 times yearly."

To make the recycling process essential and thorough, the monarch would call for the consolidation of all coinage at one place to maximize profit and to prevent competition from earlier issues (of the coins). The authorities had to make the new issues distinguishable from the earlier ones while still making the new issues widely and generally acceptable.

The wear and tear on the coins did not warrant the "recycling" of these coins; the minting profits did. The English monarch used these profits (called seigniorage) to supplement the efficient taxation systems they had adopted from the Normans. Since the value of the seigniorage depended on public perception and confidence in the minted coinage, they came up with an elaborate system of testing.

Early Forms of Counterfeit Currency Checks

In his book, *A History of Money From Ancient Times to the Present Day*, Glyn Davies says the following {non-verbatim}

"Anyone in a position that allowed him to handle silver and gold, whether that be a merchant, tax collector, the King, traders, the sheriffs, and even the royal treasury, needed to have reliable devices with which he could test the authenticity and purity of the coins that passed as currency."

Of the methods used to test this authenticity and purity was a method called rough and ready. In this method, those in the previously mentioned positions ran the coins over touchstones such as schist and quartz and examined the color traces left by the metal making the coins. The other method was a method called the Trial of the Pyx. This method involved the use of "touch needles" (24 in number, one for each of the traditional gold carats and similar test pieces of silver). The test happened before a jury.

Even though monarchs and governments had in place elaborate measures to curtail the use of counterfeits — measures such as the ones we have discussed above — counterfeits still happened despite the government being in control of coin production and the supply of money. This monopoly broke after the introduction of paper money and commercial banking.

The Introduction of Paper Money

The first use of paper money traces back to China as early as 960 AD. One reason for the need for paper money in China came about in 806-821 when, during the reign of Emperor Hien Tsung, there was a shortage of the copper used to make coinage.

Increased reliance on paper money came about when China had to exhaust its currency reserve to buy off potential invaders in the north. The result of this is that by 1020 AD, the quantity of paper money issued was so excessive that it led to inflation.

Money in the Present: Plastic Money

As you can see, our use of various forms of money throughout millennia is long. Today, although we no longer use cowry shells, and barter trade is not a common way to trade, we still use paper money and governments and monarchs the world over control monetary policies; this means that even today, our use of money is not that different from what it once was.

Today, although we still use coins and paper money, these have also taken other forms such as credit and debit cards and to some extent, wireless monies such as those held in online accounts such as PayPal. Today, credit and debit cards (what we call plastic monies) are the most commonly used form of monies (not literally) with the Federal Reserve showing that over 609.8 million credit cards are in use in the U.S. The introduction of plastic money has changed how we carry and use money.

With the first credit card (called the Diners Club card) produced in the 1950s, carrying cash and paying for things has become easier. Today, with the introduction of electronic funds transfer services such as wire transfer, paying, sending, and receiving money has become easier than it has ever been.

The introduction of the internet and its subsequent wide adoption and acceptance also brought with it a disruptive form of currency: *cryptocurrency*.

Now that you have a firm understand of how we got where we are in terms of our use of money, let us start our journey into the future by looking at how currencies of today (especially cryptocurrencies) are changing our view, understanding, and use of money in everyday life and how they will continue doing so in the future.

Section 2: Understanding the Blockchain Technology

You have brushed shoulders with terms such as Bitcoins, Litecoins, Ethereum, cryptocurrencies, and the blockchain technology. To those not in the know, these terms are confusing In this section of the guide, we shall seek to understand what these are by demystifying their underlying technology: *the blockchain technology*.

Blockchain 101: A Succinct Guide

If you look at the world we live in, one of the things you are going to note is that our world is rapidly changing. The advent of the internet brought with it a plethora of unstoppable changes. It changed the way we communicate, and more importantly, how we conduct monetary transactions.

Looking at the history of money as we have discussed it, you will realize that even in the early 20th century, the concept of sending money electronically from a computer or even mobile phones was a foreign concept. Various technological inventions have changed that. One of these technologies is the blockchain technology that brought with it the wildly popular cryptocurrency Bitcoin (we shall discuss cryptocurrencies later). For now, let us concentrate on the blockchain technology.

What is the Blockchain Technology?

According to Wikipedia, blockchain, originally called block chain, is a growing list of records called blocks secured and linked through cryptography, a form of secure communication.

Wikipedia goes further to state that each of the blocks in the blockchain has a hash pointer, a special function used to map data and link it to the previous block, a trusted timestamp that securely tracks the creation and modification of time in relation to data creation, and transaction data. This explanation tells us that a blockchain is an openly distributed, and publicly accessible, ledger used to record transactions in a way that is both verifiable and permanent.

For a blockchain ledger to be distributable, its management has to be on a peer-to-peer network that collectively adheres to a preset protocol for validating new blocks. In computing, a peer-to-peer model is a model where the architecture of the application using the model divides tasks called workload to the peers using the network. In this model, all peers have equal privileges and by connecting, they form a peer-to-peer network consisting of nodes.

The blockchain technology uses a distributed ledger. This means all the peers have open and equal access to the ledger; it also means that if a peer changes something on the ledger, the changes shall be visible to all peers since the network collectively validates the creation of new inputs within the network. Once recorded into the chain, the recorded transactions are unchangeable and an attempt to change one element of the block will lead to the alteration of all previous and subsequent blocks.

In modern day societies, the most commonly known use of the blockchain technology is as a facilitative factor in the creation and management of cryptocurrencies such as Bitcoins, Litecoins, and the likes, something we shall discuss later.

Simply stated, a blockchain is a ledger used to record transactions across many computers or a computer network. The purpose of this is to make sure that because of the peer-to-peer distribution of the ledger, no one person can covertly make changes to the ledger. The technology finds varied uses in the recording and verification of online transactions.

This very fact, the fact that they are decentralized (since no one person has explicit control over the ledger), is one of the key differences between fiat currencies (fiat currencies are government-controlled and backed legal tender such as the dollar, the pound, and most currencies of the world), and all the currencies that ride upon the blockchain technology.

The peer-to-peer aspect of the blockchain technology plays a very central role in its use. Without the peers verifying and auditing all transactions, anyone with access can alter the transactions, thereby changing all aspects of the ledger, which may lead to possible failure of the network.

For the blockchain technology to use the peer-to-peer model successfully, recording and verification of all transactions has to be relatively inexpensive. To ensure this, the technology uses mass collaboration and a collective interest for all those involved in the collation of the data into the blockchain.

In the cryptocurrencies model, one of the main uses of the blockchain technology, something changing on a daily basis as the world starts adopting the blockchain technology in other areas such as writing and health, this translates into sharing the resources created after recording a complete block, what we call mining.

In this model, the collective interest is the coins generated from recording transactions, which also leads to the creation of a new block and its residual assets—in this case, cryptocurrencies in the form of coins. The peers also share the cost levied on recording transactions. Because the participants of the peer network get rewards in the form of coins, the result is a vibrant workflow where because the network is not centralized, those using it are not overly concerned with security breaches.

One reason why the blockchain technology is finding wide adoption in the creation of cryptocurrencies and digital assets is its ability to remove infinite reproducibility from these assets. Because the purpose of the decentralized ledger is to ensure each peer plays a role in confirming that each transaction happens only once, blockchain creates a solution for double spending, a long-standing problem associated with digital assets. Many experts also describe blockchain as a value-exchange protocol where the completion of the exchange of value is cheaper and quicker than traditional systems such as wire transfers.

The database that makes up the blockchain has two kinds of records: blocks and transactions. Blocks hold sets of valid transactions hashed and cryptically encoded into a Merkle tree, which in cryptography, is a form of tree where a data block characterizes every leaf node and a cryptographic hash of the child node label characterize the non-leaf nodes. A hash tree (or many of them), allow for the secure and efficient verification of the content stored in the block.

Individual blocks have a hash of the block before it in the blockchain. This hash interlinks the two blocks. Once interlinked, the blocks form a chain; the chain makes it possible to confirm the integrity of the previous block all the way to the original block. A singular change in any of these blocks would lead to changes in all blocks created and recorded and those yet to be.

Depending on how the peers are using the blockchain (perhaps to create digital currencies or record and verify data), some blockchain based applications can create new blocks as frequently as every 5 seconds while some can take as long as 10 minutes or more. In other instances, the production of separate blocks can happen concurrently. As a blockchain ages, it also grows in height.

Other than using secure hash-based history, blockchains use a specific algorithm to score different versions of the history. The result of this is that in instances where one block has a higher value than the others, the peers can select the higher-valued block. The blocks not included in the chain end up orphaned (called orphan blocks).

Since self-interest is what drives the peers, despite having different versions of the history, peers only keep the highest scoring version of the database. When peers obtain a higher scoring version of the history, they make improvements to the database in their possession by overwriting or extending the information in it; they then share the improvements with the peer network. The greatest aspect of this is that even in instances where peers make changes to the history, the entry may not remain the same or as the best version because the peers can modify it.

By design, blockchains are secure since they use cryptography. Because they use peer-to-peer networking, they are the perfect example of distributed computing. Decentralization, a key element of the blockchain, means it finds use in many areas other than recording events. For instance, and as displayed earlier, it can prove very useful in record management, food traceability, medical records, and other areas such as identity management.

Now that we have a fair understanding of what the blockchain is, let us look at how it came into being.

History of the Blockchain

Although Satoshi Nakamoto, the creator of Bitcoin, takes home the trophy for creating the first widely accepted application using the blockchain technology, blockchain has a long history that came before him (he still takes home the trophy for creating the first usable form of blockchain. In fact, most of the applications using this technology today use what he was able to achieve as a benchmark).

In 1991, Stuart Haber and W. Scott Stornetta wrote a paper describing a cryptographically secure chain of block. In the following year, as a way to improve the efficiency of the ability to collect several of the documents into a block, the two introduced Merkle trees.

In 2008, Satoshi Nakamoto conceptualized the first distributed form of the blockchain. In the following year, he implemented it to create the currency Bitcoin. In Bitcoin, the blockchain served the purpose of being the management mechanism for the publicly distributed ledger for all financial transactions between peers. In this regard, the system used the peer-to-peer modeling and a distributed timestamp to make sure that the management of the Bitcoin database remained autonomous. The use of blockchain in the creation of Bitcoin proved the key to solving the problem of double spending, something very common with digital currencies in those days, without the need for secure administration.

In his initial paper published on 2008, Satoshi (the identity of Satoshi is still unknown. Some think he is a man living in Japan while others consider Satoshi a pseudonym for a group), used the terms block and chain on separate occasions and as separate terms. When others started using what he had achieved, they used the term block chain and in 2016, the term became one: blockchain.

In 2014, just six years after the conceptualization of Bitcoin, the first app running on the blockchain technology (Bitcoin and blockchain are not mutually exclusive and as you now know, Bitcoin is not the only use of the blockchain technology), the size of the Bitcoin blockchain stood at over 20 gigabytes. As use of the currency increased, the size of the file increased to over 30 gigabytes by January of the following year (2015), a size that had grown to over 100 gigabytes by 2017.

2014 brought with it a new term: blockchain 2.0, a term used to refer to applications (other than Bitcoin) using the blockchain technology called Ethereum. An Op-ed piece published on The Economist described the implementation of these new generation apps as follows: *"blockchain 2.0 is a sort of programming language that allows users to write sophisticated smart contracts. These smart contracts allow for the creation of invoices that pay themselves upon the arrival of a shipment or share certificates that automatically send their owners dividends if profits reach a certain level."*

While this definition is very true, application of blockchain 2.0 applications goes beyond transaction. They allow for the exchange of value on a peer-to-peer basis without the explicit need of powerful intermediaries such as banks acting as arbiters or keeping records of transactions or information. These applications allow those who would otherwise not have access to global currencies such as the dollar or pound to play an equal part in global trade and economy. Through smart contracts and cryptography, these platforms also foster privacy protection (which is why in its early days, criminals on the Silk Road website used Bitcoin as their preferred means of trade).

Applications that use blockchain 2.0 make the storage of a person's individual ID and persona easier and secure; because of this, they are helping shape future monies, distribution of wealth, and ease wealth inequality.

A Chronological Development of Blockchain Related Technologies

We cannot fail to mention that in the 10 years the blockchain innovation has been in existence, it has gone through some changes and seen the introduction of various new technologies that have made it what it is today. Here is a chronological view of these changes:

1. The first major innovation of the technology occurred when Satoshi introduced Bitcoin, the first successful application to use the blockchain technology. Introduced in a world in dire need of a decentralized currency, wide adoption of Bitcoins has seen their market cap rise to over $20 billion. Today, thousands of people across the world are using this blockchain-based currency to make payments and online purchases.

2. After the development of Bitcoin came the realization that the underlying technology could apply to many other areas and that the technology itself was not synonymous with Bitcoins. Many world-leading financial institutions are currently researching how they can integrate the technology into their financial offerings and in-house applications. According to research by Fortune.com, about 15% of all major banks are looking into how they can integrate the technology into their processes.

3. The third major innovation in blockchain development was the introduction of smart contracts. Simply put, a smart contract is a computer-based protocol whose aim is to facilitate, enforce, and verify contractual negotiations. Of all smart contracts introduced, the Ethereum blockchain platform is the most prominent one; we shall discuss its development and application later. Ethereum built multiple, 2nd gen programs into the blockchain platform to allow for the transfer of loans, bonds, and other financial instruments. The development of Ethereum came out of necessity.

4. The 4th innovation, which is what many blockchain 2.0 applications in existence today use, is proof of stake. Applications such as Bitcoin (the current version of it), use something called proof of work. In the blockchain world, proof of work is data that is easy to verify based on certain requirements but that is difficult or costly to produce. Proof of work produced the aspect of mining where a computer or group of networked computers with the most computing power would make the decisions in that since they had the most power, they could provide secure proof of work faster for all blockchain transactions such as cryptocurrencies transfers or payments. For their services, these computers earn cryptocurrencies; this explains why cryptocurrency mining has become popular.

These four are the main developmental stages of blockchain. Experts also agree that in the days to come, another revolutionary innovation that is going to change the blockchain technology is blockchain scaling. Here is how this shall pan out.

We have already established that a blockchain is a decentralized, peer-to-peer managed ledger upon which the transactions recorded by the computers on the network reside. As we have also seen, processing these transactions uses the computing power of every computer in the network, something that has proven slow and rather expensive to manage (which is why cryptocurrency mining is not as lucrative as it once used to be).

Because of the above, blockchain scaling, a new form of blockchain innovation, is on the horizon. This innovation intends to accelerate the rate at which the computers on the network record the data into blocks, all this without sacrificing the security or integrity of the block. To do this, blockchain scaling intends to interrogate the network to determine the number of computers needed to validate individual transactions and using this base number, divide the work equally among all the computers in the network. As you can imagine, this will lead to increased efficiency. This technology, if it comes to fruition, which is likely to be very soon, will rival technologies such as SWIFT and VISA, and play an integral role in powering the internet of things.

The above is a representation of how blockchain has changed in the last 10 years thanks to the work of an elite group of mathematicians, cryptographers, and computer scientists working to improve this disruptive innovation. As the innovation continues to improve, it is changing many things about how we live our everyday life. For instance, many experts in the field opine that as these breakthroughs come through, the future may see us using blockchain technologies to pay for services such as charging stations and landing pads for self-driving cars and drones.

Now that we are talking about how the blockchain technology is changing the future of money, we cannot fail to discuss Ethereum, the other blockchain innovation that is changing our perception of the blockchain as a predominantly currency-development technology. Before we do that, however, let us discuss the benefits of the blockchain technology.

Benefits of the Blockchain Technology

Other than being the backbone upon which cryptocurrencies such as Bitcoin rest, the blockchain technology has a vast number of uses whose benefits surpasses that of cryptocurrencies and their creation. Let us discuss some of these benefits before we discuss Ethereum in the next section.

The need for blockchain is not as evident as it would be because as many postulate, you can use a software or platform such as Google or databases to record transactions. While databases have no fault, blockchain has proven effectual and beneficial. Here are some of its key benefits:

Fully Distributed

This is one of the key benefits of the blockchain technology. As illustrated many times in this guide, participants in any blockchain application, perhaps Bitcoin mining or trading, will have access to a copy of the most current blockchain.

Mining of the currencies that use these technologies is also distributed. This means that at any point in time, no computer (no matter how powerful it is) can dominate the network. If that were the case, the most powerful computers would do all the mining and hog all the created currencies leaving none for the hobby miner. The distributed nature of the blockchain makes this impossible.

Use of Decentralized Verification

We have discussed how currencies and applications that use the blockchain technology are decentralized. This aspect of the innovation eliminates the need for a central authority such as a central bank; having to take transactions through a central database can be limiting in terms of the time it takes for the transaction to happen.

Enhanced Security

In a widely corrupt internet where some people use blackhat strategies to trick users into giving them their bank and credit card information, an anonymous way of paying for goods and services proves very helpful. Since many online buyers are seeking anonymity above all else, they are turning to blockchain powered currencies such as Bitcoins and Ether since these currencies use cryptographically secure, complex algorithms to record all transactions without compromising personal identity. To make and receive blockchain-powered currencies, all you need is an address. This reduces the risk of fraud.

Enhanced Trust among Parties

Blockchain offers top-level security features (using cryptographic code). This increases the level of trust between those transacting. Further, because there is zero exchange of value, and records of the transactions remain on the blockchain under all circumstances, the level of trust between those sending cryptocurrencies and those receiving it increases.

Low Entry Barrier

This is one of the key benefits of the blockchain innovation: it allows anyone to use the network—anyone who has an internet connected computer or smartphone can use blockchain and Bitcoins as long as he or she downloads the client software.

Real-time Transactional Capabilities

Waiting for three or more days for a transaction to reflect on your bank or account statement is a pain many users are keen to avoid whenever they can —today's consumers want immediate results after making any purchase: they want the transaction to reflect on their accounts almost immediately.

The blockchain technology makes it possible to make payments immediately or within 10 minutes, which when you consider the time it takes for credit cards to process transactions, is the best option currently available.

Enhanced Global Operations and Trade

Considering that we live in an interconnected world where someone in America can be in business with someone living at the farthest point in Africa, the need for speedy transactions has never been higher. Blockchain based currencies enhance this intercontinental trade by enhancing the speed of transactions and reducing the fees levied on sending monies from one person or business to the other.

Eliminates the Problem of Double Spending

This is something we discussed earlier as one of the key advantages of the blockchain technology. We have also mentioned that applications using the blockchain use cryptography to secure the system and prevent the duplication of transaction (especially monetary ones) to make sure that users of the system do not produce money out of thin air.

The system processes each transaction once before entering it into a block and linking the block to the chain. Once processed and recorded into the blockchain, the system cannot process that transaction again; this eliminates the redundancy so common with the records of most modern banking systems. Further, because the arrangement of the blocks uses a linear and chronological manner, tracking transactions becomes dummy-easy.

Low Transaction Costs

One of the main reasons why the uptake of cryptocurrencies such as Bitcoins and Litecoins has been on the rapid rise is the fact that most of these currencies have the lowest transfer rates imaginable. This plays in very well with consumers who are looking to save money on transactional fees as they shop.

The links below show how to calculate transactional fees for ether and Bitcoins.

https://ethereum.stackexchange.com/questions/19665/how-to-calculate-transaction-fee

https://en.bitcoin.it/wiki/Transaction_fees

https://bitcoinfees.21.co/

Those advocating for, and spearheading the use of, the blockchain technology are quick to point out that the applicability of the innovation goes beyond that of Bitcoin or financial transactions. For instance, many of those involved are quick to point out that the blockchain shall play an integral role in elections of the future (read more here).

Still, like every new technology, there are those who feel that the technology has its fair share of drawbacks, especially its ability to accommodate the rapid uptake and increased number of transactions. Since most applications that use this technology create an average of 61 new blocks every 10 minutes, each individual system creates an average of 144 blocks per day. To the cautious, this is something they consider problematic because it may influence the storage and speed of transaction, which may lead to update and synchronization issues.

Let us flesh out some of the drawbacks of the blockchain technology and discuss their possible solutions:

Disadvantages of Using Blockchain Technology

While the blockchain has many uses and an immense number of benefits, it also has its drawbacks. In this subsection, we shall look at these disadvantages as well as how to overcome them:

Performance

The first issue many are quick to point out is the issue of performance. Some experts in the field of finance point out that compared to the speed of centralized databases especially in relation to transaction records, the blockchain is slower because on top of recording a transaction as a normal database does, it also has to do three other things:

1. Verify signature: Every blockchain transaction must have a digital signature that uses a public-private cryptographic scheme (a good example is the ECDSA signature). Without this signature, it would be impossible to prove the source of transactions propagated on the nodes of the peer-to-peer network. As you can guess, generating and verifying these signatures requires a massive amount of computer power and, since the signatures are complex, their computation may take time thus slowing down the recording of transactions. In comparison, centralized databases (normal ones) do not have to contend with this problem because after the establishment of a connection with the databases, it eliminates the need for individual verification of requests coming over it.

Possible solution: A possible solution for this is the move to proof-of-stake, which would make transactions faster while eliminating the need to have nodes on the network verify individual transactions.

2. Consensus Mechanism: One of the key characteristic of the blockchain is that it monitors the nodes (computers) on the network and, using some of the computing power of the network, makes sure the nodes within the network reach consensus. Achieving this consensus means there has to be a significant back-and-forth communication between all the nodes and may involve dealing with forks and their effects on the blockchain. This may cause a slowdown of transaction procession. While traditional centralized databases also have to contend with aborted and conflicting transactions, because the database is centralized, these are few.

Possible solution: The consensus mechanism is all about proof-of-work. As the system moves away from proof-of-work to proof-of-stake, it is bound to remove the hindrances that come with it.

The links below detail critical information about the various consensus mechanisms used by various blockchain applications:

https://www.linkedin.com/pulse/types-consensus-mechanism-used-blockchain-munish-singh/

https://bitmalta.com/blockchain-consensus/

3. Redundancy: In this regard, redundancy does not necessarily mean the performance of individual nodes on the network; it means the amount of computing power required to compute a blockchain. Every node on the blockchain network must process every node individually, something that does not

plague centralized databases that process individual transactions just ones. On the blockchain network, this means more work for the same results, which as you can guess, leads to slowed down processes.

Possible solution: Again, most blockchain application and technologies use proof-of-work to verify transactions. A move to proof-of-stake and other consensus mechanism would eliminate this and take with it the drawbacks.

To learn more about the average time it takes the blockchain network to record transactions, read the insightful content on the links below.

https://coincenter.org/entry/how-long-does-it-take-for-a-bitcoin-transaction-to-be-confirmed

https://bitcoin.stackexchange.com/questions/7323/how-long-does-it-take-on-average-to-receive-one-confirmation-is-it-still-revers

Energy

Many have touted the blockchain technology as the answer to global warming because it provides a transparent currency not based on consumption. Some opine that the innovation as currently instituted — where computer nodes spread across the world have to record all transaction using proof-of-work —leaves a massive carbon imprint because all the computers on the network have to use energy. In fact, some experts are quick to point out that the peer-to-peer power used to process Bitcoins is superior to that of the world's fastest computers combined.

Possible Solution: A possible solution to this is to move away from proof-of-work, thereby eliminating the need for mining, and move to other consensus mechanisms that do not require combined computing power. While this solution may not be forthcoming anytime soon, it shall, and when it does, it shall change everything.

The other solution is a tradeoff between security and size where those spearheading the development of the technology can trade security for size. The downside to this is that the more nodes you have on the network, the more secure it is; however, in an instance where you only want part of the data on the blockchain, perhaps having a smaller, yet faster network would be better. This means that institutions such as banks can set up their smaller blockchain networks and by so doing, save on energy costs, and increase the rate of transaction recording.

Interoperability

Interoperability, making sure that the network and the data therein has standards and is not a bunch of stuff, is a growing concern. Since blockchain technology is open-source and anyone can use it to create whatever blockchain application he or she wants while tweaking it accordingly, there are no set standards for the technology, and competing blockchain platforms are free to use it as they wish. The individual changes and tweaks make it impossible for competing blockchain technologies to achieve a level of interoperability.

Possible solution: A possible solution for this would be for all blockchain-based app developers to achieve consensus and make their individual blockchain applications compatible with the wider web; they can do this by integrating their apps into existing processes and practices.

Privacy

Although most applications using the blockchain technology as their backbone use cryptography to secure data, privacy is a key concern since the blockchain is a publicly visible ledger. This level of openness is not what anyone would consider the most secure way to store sensitive data.

As an example, the Bitcoin blockchain/database has a record of all transactions ever conducted on the platform. This data is open for all to see, which also means anyone can use the same data against someone else. A case in point is the Department of Work and Pension. In May 2016, they started using the blockchain to track how claimants use their benefits.

When you consider that when you conduct transactions over the Bitcoin blockchain, you are publishing your bank statement online for all to see, privacy concerns are sure to arise.

Possible Solution: A possible solution for this would be to use complex cryptographic code to make sure that the transactions are secure and no one can game the system or use the information therein to disadvantage someone else. Another possible solution would be Bitcoin mixing.

The following link has some great ideas on how to enhance privacy over the Bitcoin blockchain (the principles also apply to other blockchain technologies).

https://coinsutra.com/anonymous-bitcoin-transactions/

Changing Truths

The blockchain operates on the premise that all information recorded into it is eternal truth and shall remain so. Reality, as you very well know, is greyer than that. In fact, some jurisdictions such as the EU and the UK have laws detailing the right to be forgotten. For instance, in the UK, if you change your gender, it is your right to have the same reflect all through history (records of birth, baptism, etc.).

If a governmental institution that offers governmental services such as birth records uses a blockchain ledger, that would mean changing such information would be impossible and doing so would lead to the creation of a fork, as was the case with the DAO project.

Encryption

One of the main points we have impressed repeatedly is that most applications on the blockchain technology use cryptography to encrypt information. This encryption creates a number of issues. For one, anyone with a key — perhaps a super user such as the person responsible for creating the specific blockchain application, someone who knows its inner working modalities — can access the encrypted data (so can anyone if the key becomes public). The other issue is that if someone loses the key that unlocks the blockchain, that blockchain would be worthless and difficult, if not impossible to get back.

As the hack on the DAO project proved, encryption, no matter how strong it is, is vulnerable either through the exploitation of backdoors and loopholes, or using new technologies. For instance, even with the immense power of peer-to-peer computing, a technology such as quantum computing (once developed), can knock the bejeezus out of the peer-to-peer network and overpower it, thus making it vulnerable.

Therefore, saying we can use cryptography to encrypt the data in the blockchain may not be enough in itself since people will always be looking for ways to de-encrypt encrypted data.

Possible Solution: A possible solution for this would be to make sure that the key that unlocks an encrypted blockchain does not fall into the wrong hands (meaning it should not be public, which in itself presents a problem seeing how the blockchain is an open ledger).

Another solution for this is to implement strong privacy protection laws and strategies. The link below has some invaluable insight into this:

https://github.com/ethereum/wiki/wiki/Problems

Illegal Entries

Consider an instance where someone with malicious intent embeds illegal data into a blockchain. That would make the entire blockchain illegal. It would also mean that anyone on the blockchain would be guilty of breaking the law and therefore culpable.

For instance, James Smith, ODI's Head of Labs Programme and co-author of a report named 'Applying Blockchain Technology in Global Data Infrastructure,' added an illegal encryption key for HD DVD on the PlayStation to the blockchain. To date, no one cares about this and the blockchain upon which the illegal encryption key rests is on everyone's' machine.

Discovering Information

The blockchain database has in place ways to record data (through the computation power of the nodes on the network). However, usage of the data is not as easy since to use the data, you have to find the data you intend to use.

While it is possible to index the blockchain into searchable databases, finding specific information in a reliable manner would require that those participating in the network have the same blockchain history stored on their nodes and a capable search index built from this blockchain. Achieving a distributed search index is something the technology is yet to explore.

Possible solution: A possible solution for information discovery would be to have one site having a search index for the chain. This may lead to possible issues as well since not many would be willing to trust that one site. The lasting solution would be to integrate a capable search feature into the blockchain.

The following links list a number of other blockchain related problems and their possible solutions:

https://appliedblockchain.com/outstanding-challenges-in-blockchain-2017/

https://www.coindesk.com/information/blockchains-issues-limitations/

https://www.kaspersky.com/blog/bitcoin-blockchain-issues/18019/

https://techcrunch.com/2016/02/03/lets-be-honest-about-the-problems-with-blockchain-and-finance/

Now that we have hashed out the possible shortcomings of the blockchain, let us discuss Ethereum, the other blockchain technology that is taking the world by storm and after that, discuss how you can start using the blockchain.

Section 3: Ethereum Guide for Beginners

Earlier, we mentioned that the perceived failures of the blockchain technology as used to create Bitcoin are what led to the creation of Ethereum. What is Ethereum and is it the same as Bitcoin? Let us look at this:

Understanding Ethereum

First off, Ethereum is not a new technology per se; as far as definitions go, Ethereum is an open-source and public, (meaning anyone can use the underlying source code and technology), blockchain-based, and distributed computing platform that uses a scripting functionality called smart contracts.

As implied earlier, a smart contract, a technology first proposed by Nick Szabo in 1996, is a computer protocol whose intent is to facilitate, enforce, and verify the performance or negotiation of a contract; the Ethereum blockchain platform accounts for its most prominent implementation.

Going back to Ethereum, the decentralized technology offers the Ethereum Virtual Machine (EVM), a virtual machine that has the capabilities to offer Turing-completeness, which in computability theory, is a system of data-manipulation rules, and the ability to execute these data-manipulation rules (scripts) using an international network of public nodes.

Since it uses the blockchain technology (and to motivate those participating in the peer-to-peer network), Ethereum also offers ether, a form of cryptocurrency that is very much like Bitcoin (meaning it is transferable) and used to compensate those participating in the computation of nodes. To mitigate spam and adequately allocate resources to the computers on the network, the platform uses an internal pricing mechanism called Gas.

How Ethereum Developed

The question of how Ethereum came into being is likely to manifest anytime two or more people are discussing the developmental stages of the blockchain technology. As we hinted at earlier, Ethereum developed primarily because of the perceived shortcomings of the blockchain technology as used to create Bitcoins.

The first mention of Ethereum is in a paper authored in 2013 by Vitalik Buterin, a programmer involved in the development of Bitcoin (he co-founded the Bitcoin Magazine, an online Bitcoin news website, worked for Egora, and coded for Dark Wallet).

Vitalik argues that his desire to develop the platform came from the need to have an integrated scripting language in the blockchain technology to allow for the development of decentralized applications. After failing to gain agreement on the inclusion of the same within the existing blockchain technology as used to create Bitcoins, he developed Ethereum, a platform that had a more generalized scripting language.

Contrary to popular belief, Ethereum and Bitcoin are not the same thing (as discussed above, Ethereum has an internal currency called ether). While the two are the same in that they are both publicly distributed blockchain networks, their purpose and capability differs substantially.

Bitcoin is but one application of the blockchain technology; it allows peer-to-peer electronic cash transfers (think of the blockchain technology as an onion and Bitcoin as one layer of the onion). While the Bitcoin blockchain uses the technology to track ownership and transference of cryptocurrencies, the Ethereum blockchain platform focuses on running decentralized applications. In the latter, on top of mining for ether, the internal cryptocurrency in Ethereum, peers intent on mining offer their computing power and in return, earn ether. Other than trading this cryptocurrency, app developers use it to pay transaction fees and services on the Ethereum network.

To learn more about what Ethereum is and its purpose, read the following helpful resource:

https://www.coindesk.com/information/what-is-ethereum/

How Ethereum Works

Having discussed what Ethereum is and how it came into being, let us move a step further and discuss its inner working modalities.

We have established that Ethereum aims to create decentralized apps, which it does using a tweaked version of the blockchain used by the bitcoin protocol; this tweak opens the platform and gives it use that surpasses the monetary use as is common in Bitcoins.

Using the Turing-completeness model, Ethereum aims to help developers create applications similar to how Bitcoins work with the only difference being that it allows developers to create new additional steps, rules of ownership, and alternate transactional formats and transfer states. This allows developers to create more programs or applications where blockchain transactions govern and to some extent, automate specific outcomes.

To demystify how this works, we need to go a step further and describe how smart contracts, something often shrouded in mystery, work:

How Smart Contracts Work

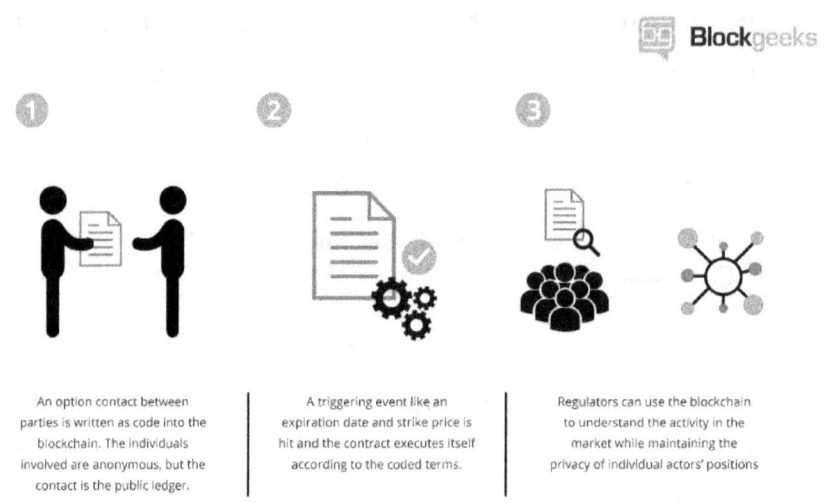

Blockgeeks

1	2	3
An option contact between parties is written as code into the blockchain. The individuals involved are anonymous, but the contact is the public ledger.	A triggering event like an expiration date and strike price is hit and the contract executes itself according to the coded terms.	Regulators can use the blockchain to understand the activity in the market while maintaining the privacy of individual actors' positions

Image courtesy of Blockgeeks.com

From a general perspective, the work of a general contract is to outline the modalities of a working relationship. For instance, if you hire a contractor, the contract you sign will outline the terms that govern the working relationship. Simply put, a smart contract is similar to this with the difference being it uses cryptographic code to enforce the terms of the contract. In other words, a smart contract is a program that works (executes) as set up by the creator/s of the contract.

Consider the following:

When using normal currencies such as credit cards to transfer money online, you have to pay through an intermediary and pay the intermediary for offering the service. This hindrance is one the blockchain technology eliminates thanks to its decentralization.

The smart contract is the brain child of Nick Szabo, a cryptographer, who in 1994 realized that the decentralized ledger could find use for smart contracts also called blockchain contracts, self-executing contracts, or digital contracts. Szabo hypothesized that it was possible to convert these contracts into cryptographically secure computer code and then store and replicate them on a system supervised by a network of computers running the blockchain.

Smart contracts facilitate the exchange of money, shares, property, and other things of value in a transparent (publicly accessible) manner that is free from the interference of intermediaries such as banks (and the fees they charge). A simpler way to describe smart contracts is by comparing them to our normal way of payment.

Assume you are in need of the services of a lawyer or accountant. Here is what normally happens; you pay for the service and then wait to receive the documentation. Smart contracts change this; when you make a payment through a digital currency such as ether or Bitcoin, you drop the coin into the ledger and immediately after, you get the service (and the papers) in your account with almost immediate effect. The smart contract automatically enforces the agreement within the contract. The Ethereum platform specifically works on the tenets of smart contracts.

Worth noting is that Bitcoins were the first to offer basic smart contracts since they allowed for the transference of value from one person to the other and since the bitcoin network only validates transactions when they meet certain conditions.

Consider the following image:

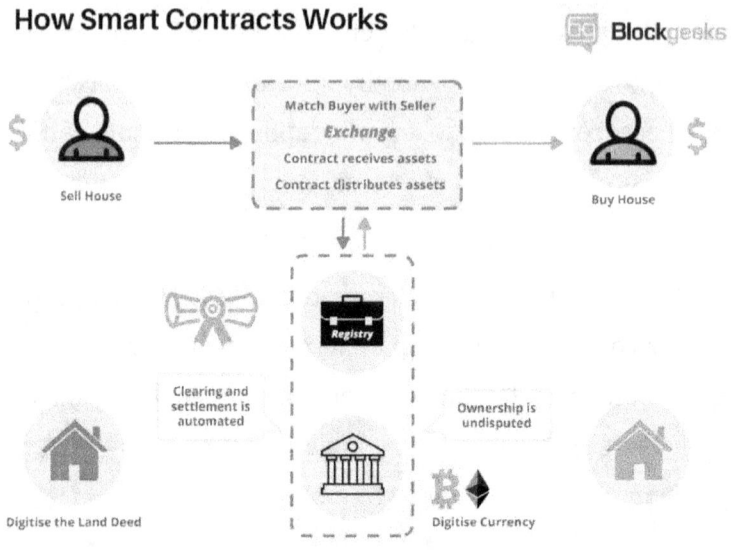

Image courtesy of Blockgeeks.com

Since Ethereum allows for the creation of smart contracts, or, as the Ethereum white paper calls them, autonomous agents, and using the Turing-complete feature, it offers support for a broader set of computational instructions. For instance, smart contracts can:

1. Manage agreements between users in an instance where one user buys something such as car or home insurance from the other user.

2. Offer a function similar to multi-signature accounts that require authorization from a specific percentage of people before the use of the funds therein.

3. Act as a utility to other contracts.

4. Act as an information storage platform for applications. For

instance, it can store the registration information for domain registration or membership records.

In relation to point 4 above, many experts in the field believe smart contracts will be codependent to some degree. For instance, placing a bet on the temperature of a cold winter day may trigger a sequence of other contracts. It may trigger a smart contract that would determine the weather, and yet another to settle the bet depending on the information received from the contract that determined the weather. Running each of these contracts would require a smart code and the execution of each contract attracts ether transactional fees. The Ethereum Virtual Machine fails to execute smart contracts that do not have enough transaction fees.

Going back to the Ethereum blockchain, we cannot fail to mention that its structure is very similar to that of the Bitcoin blockchain in that both store and publicly share all transactions recorded, and every node (or computer) on the network has a copy of this records history.

The main difference between the Bitcoin and Ethereum blockchains is that instead of storing the entire history on each node (computer), each node of the Ethereum blockchain stores the state of the most recent smart contract and all ether transactions. It tracks the user balance, the smart code contract, and its storage location. In comparison, to track how many Bitcoins someone possesses, the bitcoin blockchain protocol uses unspent transaction outputs.

While this may sound overly complex, the underlying idea is relatively simple. Whenever someone makes a Bitcoin transaction, the bitcoin protocol breaks up the total amount and issues back change where necessary much in the same way physical coins or paper money behaves. For future transactions, the network has to add all the pieces of change classified as spent or unspent. This is one of the key differences between the Ethereum and bitcoin blockchains: the Ethereum one uses accounts. Ether tokens are much like funds in a bank account (from an appearance perspective), and are thus portable to another account or wallet without having what we would call a continued relationship.

When talking about this, we cannot fail to mention the applications of smart contracts.

The Application Possibilities for Smart Contracts

While smart contracts have their fair share of problems, problems such as buggy code, governmental reaction to such decentralization, and the uncertainty over what would happen if someone hacked the network (like what happened with the Ethereum network after the DAO event and the eventual creation of Ethereum classic), they are also wildly beneficial.

Some of the key benefits they offer include autonomy, trust, backup and security, speed, savings on transactions, and accuracy. These benefits make smart contracts a technology deployable in many areas. Some of the key areas that are either using or are eager to use smart contracts include:

Governmental Use

There is consensus that while the digital voting system in the United States is hard to rig, there is also growing concern over this after claims that the Russian government hacked the election system during the 2016 U.S. elections.

Smart contracts can allay this fear in that their core system is a security-based one. By using smart contracts, anyone looking to hack and manipulate the ledger-protected votes would need excessively high computing power, a feat no one could manage since no one has computing power that would exceed the combined computing power of the peer-to-peer connected computers that run the blockchain network.

The other point of note here is that since a voting application using the smart contracts model would eliminate the need to show your identity and complete the voting forms, the voting process would be faster, which would lead to an increase in voter turnout since the system would be relatively easy to use.

Management

The single ledger aspect of the blockchain technology is a source of trust (since changes on one end would reflect on all aspects of the ledger). Other than that, the transparency, accuracy, and autonomy it offers would improve communication and workflow. When you consider that a lack of communication and workflow are some of the key hindrances to business productivity and success, an immediate approval of internal issues and the elimination of the back-and-forth that makes up the business environment would lead to an improved business environment.

A case in point here is the Depository Trust and Clearing Corp (DTCC). In 2015, they used the blockchain ledger to process 345 million transactions representing more than $1.5 quadrillion of securities.

Supply chain

At the heart of smart contracts is the If-Then premise. For instance, if the weather is X, then execute bet Y or so. Jeff Garzik, a key contributor to Bitcoin core and the co-founder of bloqinc puts it as follows:

"UPS can execute contracts that say, 'If I receive cash on delivery at this location in a developing, emerging market, then this other [product], many, many links up the supply chain, will trigger a supplier creating a new item since the existing item was just delivered in that developing market.'" All too often, paper-based systems where forms have to pass through numerous channels for approval hamper supply chains and increase exposure to loss and fraud. The blockchain nullifies this by providing a secure, accessible digital version to all parties on the chain and automates tasks and payment."

A case study of this is Barclays Corporate Bank; it uses smart contracts to record change of ownership and the automatic transfer of payment to other financial institutions.

Automobile

Our technology is rapidly developing and in the future, everything promises to be autonomous (think along the line of smart cars, smart drones, and the likes). In this future, smart contracts will prove very useful.

As an example, smart contracts will play a very central role in the self-parking of autonomous vehicles in that from an overall perspective and in the case of an accident, they will help authorities determine who was at fault, the driver, the sensors, or other variables. Using the smart contract protocol, an automobile insurance could use a driver's history to determine the rate at which to charge a premium.

Real Estate

Consider the normal way of handling real estate deals. If you want to rent out your house or apartment, you have to go through an intermediary, an online ad placement platform such as Craigslist, or hire a real estate agent. This means you would have to pay that someone or advertising platform. You would also have to hire someone to make sure that the tenant keeps up the payments.

A smart contract eliminates the need for this; all you have to do is pay via a cryptocurrency and encode your contract into the ledger. This would allow for automatic fulfilment and provide a level of openness. This would benefit all involved: brokers, real estate agents, and even the proprietor.

Healthcare

The blockchain technology makes it possible to encode and store personal health records using a private key that would grant access to individuals specified within the contract. This means the system would enable the storage of research, medical reports, and receipts (perhaps surgery receipts) in a safe and secure manner whereby using the If-Then protocol, the system would automatically dispatch the file to insurance providers (as proof-of-delivery) and to all those involved, perhaps a GP offering general health management, drug use supervision and regulation, labs, etc.

Now that we have a clearer understanding of what Ethereum is, and how smart contracts work, let us discuss how Ethereum mining works.

Mining: How Mining Works

It is very easy to confuse the purpose of Ethereum mining. In fact, many of those new to the Ethereum innovation are quick to conclude that mining is all about generating ether without the need for a central issuer. While there is truth to this, especially since the process of mining leads to the creation of new Ethereum tokens (ether) — at a rate of 5 ethers per mined block — mining plays another important role.

In our modern world, our banks have the mandate of keeping accurate transactional records. They also play the role of ensuring that the monies transferred from one account to the other does not happen twice, thereby leading to the creation of money from thin air. Blockchain changes this working modality and the maintenance of records by ensuring that the records kept are not under the supervisory authority of an intermediary; it makes the process of record keeping and verification public in a publicly held ledger. Mining ensures the system is secure, and that no one cheats or uses previously used monies again (the problem of double spending solved through the proof of work concept). Miners play the important role of maintaining transaction history to prevent fraud.

The Ethereum mining process is very similar to the Bitcoin mining process. Here is how both work. Miners use very powerful computers (in terms of computing power) to guess the answer to the puzzle that makes up each transaction block. This happens at lighting fast speeds until one of these computers guesses right.

To be a bit more specific, these miners use a hash function to run the unique header metadata of the block (including the timestamp and the software version). The result of this is a fixed-length string of randomly looking numbers and letter; the system only changes the nonce value, which affects the resulting hash value.

When a miner finds a hash matching the current target, that miner receives an award of ether (or Bitcoins) and then broadcasts the solved block to every computer on network (what we have called nodes before) for validation and addition to their ledger. To take this a step further, if miner X solves the hash puzzle, everyone working on that block stops working on that block and starts working on the next block. Since computers are the ones doing this work, this happens automatically. This system is very difficult to cheat because it requires proof-of-work and there is no way to fake the correct answer to the puzzle that unlocks the hash/block.

On the Ethereum blockchain, the discovery of a new block takes approximately 12-15 seconds (10 minutes for Bitcoins). When miners solve the puzzle quicker or slower than this rate, the intuitive algorithm automatically changes the difficulty of the mathematical puzzle with the intent being to get miners back to the 12-seconds solution time. Once created and solved, it takes very little time for all miners/nodes or computers on the network to verify the correctness of the hash value. How many ethers or Bitcoins a miner earns depends on the miner's computing power (the more the power, the higher the ether probability).

Ethereum uses a proof-of-work algorithm called ethash; this algorithm specifically requires more memory, which makes solving the mathematical hash puzzle harder and miners have to use specialized, highly powerful computers called ASICs, computers that have special mining chips.

Another important thing to note here is that Ethereum mining may change in the future as Ethereum shifts from using proof-of-work to using proof-of-stake. Let us briefly discuss proof-of-stake.

Shifting to Proof of Stake

As stated, Ethereum is moving away from proof-of-work and leaning towards proof of stake. This means in the future Ethereum will not need miners.

Proof-of-work is the algorithm currently used to determine the validity of transactions and keep the ledger secure. Proof of stake will see the network secured by owners of tokens. Once rolled out, proof-of-stake will eliminate the need for mining rigs and immense computing power. It will allow for the distribution of the ledger using fewer resources.

Now that we have discussed these things, let us discuss how you can start using the blockchain technology.

Section 4: A Technical Guide to Getting Started on Blockchain

As the title suggests, this section is going to focus on how you can get started on implementing blockchain. As you can guess, applying blockchain will be multi-faceted and as such. We shall have to look at how you can implement the innovation into your business and how you can start developing blockchain driven apps. Later — in section 5 — we shall discuss how to get your hands on cryptocurrencies and start trading them for profit. For now, let us start our discussions on how to get started on blockchain.

Getting Started On Blockchain: Implementing Blockchain into Business Operations

Throughout our discussion thus far, we have discussed how the blockchain technology has many practical uses in everyday life. Some of the key uses we detailed apply to businesses, which is what we shall discuss in this section of the guide.

Whether you run a small business or an enterprise level one, you are always on the lookout for technologies that can increase your efficiency and help you grow your business. As such, you may be eager to integrate blockchain into your business operation if not for the profits, to minimize the drawbacks of using a centralized system of record management.

However, before you think of implementing this technology into your business, you have to ask yourself if the technology will meet your business needs. This question deserves an honest and very succinct answer because as you will see shortly, blockchain is not a one size fits all solution and, contrary to popular belief, it is not an optimal solution to all business processes.

The blockchain technology is useful in very specific niche use cases. In these niche use cases, the solution they provide is top level and elegant. Some of these niche uses include the following (use this list to determine where you can implement the technology within your business):

1. Audit: If your desire is to have a process that records business processes in a tamper-proof way, then this technology will suit you well because as we have stated, once entered into the

blockchain, changing entries becomes difficult and doing so means the changed entry will be visible for all to see. This can prove very helpful for audit purposes.

2. Data Transfer or Proof of Data Storage: If you want to have a system that allows you to know with certainty when a specific author created a document (and the identity of the author), this technology will prove very useful because the nodes on the network will record such details and make them publicly accessible to all using the network.

3. Transfer of Assets: If your business is looking for a way to transfer digital assets in an instantaneous manner that leaves an audit trail, thereby eliminating dependence and the need for authorization from third parties, this technology shall also prove very useful. The cost of transferring these assets will also prove very beneficial to your business's health since its low-cost.

Using these three points, determine if your business can successfully implement blockchain technology into your operations. In addition to these, also consider the artificial rules and controls of centralization, vulnerability to errors, hacking, internal fraud, points of failure, and trapped capital.

After determining that your business can benefit from this technology, the next step is to determine how to integrate the technology into your existing business infrastructure. To do this, you have to integrate your blockchain application of choice in conjunction with the existing system (parallel) as you test out the technology in the niche use.

Testing your preferred blockchain application can be as simple accessing an Application Programming Interface (API) to access the blockchain protocol, and while there does exist various advanced ways to use blockchain, ways that require financial and resource investment, accessing the API will do for now especially if you are in the testing phase. The best solution would be to inform yourself about the capabilities of the blockchain and then conduct a small internal test in a niche area of your organization.

Blockchain-Based Applications You Can Integrate Into Your Business

Continuing with the above discussion, here are the various technologies that have blockchain capabilities and that you can integrate into your business:

Blockchain Distributed Cloud Storage

In the next 2-5 years, blockchain data storage is going to be a massively disruptive technology that will upset the current status quo where cloud storage adopts the centralized model (think back to how you have trusted Google or Amazon cloud storage to keep your data safe).

The blockchain can allow you to store and distribute information you would otherwise entrust to a third party thereby decentralizing it (and probably slashing the cost of data storage). Storj, a decentralized, in beta-testing, blockchain powered cloud storage platform is the best example of this. The platform improves security, decreases dependency on third parties, and allows you to rent out your excess storage capacity.

Digital Identity

Digital security, i.e. about vulnerability to hacking, is a key business concern; blockchain can lay this concern to bed. The technology does so by making sure that managing and tracking digital identities is safe and effectual. This reduces the risk of fraud.

The critical thing here is that digital identity verification and authorization weaves into services such as online banking and transactions, national security and citizenship documentation, and even things such email sign in.

Hacking of databases and cloud storage spaces such as iCloud are common (Target was the recent target of a broad and significant breach—the breach compromised information of over 70 million customers).

You can use blockchain to secure your digital identities in a process that would require a unique authentication of identities in a way that is both secure and irrefutable. Considering that current identity identification methods are password based, using blockchain would make the process secure since it would use a digital signature based on a public, cryptographically secured key. In this setup, the only requirement that would determine the authenticity of an identity would be checking if the correct private key signed the transaction. Blockchain identity application can apply to passports, birth and wedding certificates, digital identities, IDs, and E-residency.

An example of such a technology in use today is ShoCard, a digital identity that offers consumer privacy protection. ShoCard is easy to use and optimized for mobile.

Blockchain Notary

Timestamp is one of the key features of the blockchain. The system validates the state of a hash (a wrapped piece of data) at specific times. This confirms the existence of something. Manuel Aráoz, a Buenos Aires blockchain developer developed proof of existence, a decentralized meth0d of verification and by so doing disrupted centralized notary services that were the only ones offering the services. He explains proof of existence as follows:

"As the blockchain is a public database, it is a distributed sort of consensus; your document becomes certified in a distributed sort of way."

Proof of existence works as follows: it enables different users to actually upload a file (securely) and, by paying a fee, have a cryptographic proof of it included in the Bitcoin blockchain. After doing this anonymously, the system generates a hash of the digital file as part of the transaction. This stores proof of your file in the public ledger without revealing your identity. Aráoz says the following about this:

"Basically, by inserting the cryptographic hash of the document in a transaction, when that transaction is mined into a block, the block timestamp becomes the record's timestamp,"

We have looked at the various ways to integrate blockchain into your business. With that understanding, let us look at how to get started on Ethereum blockchain and the development of smart contracts.

Smart Contract and Ethereum Web Development: A Practical Getting-started Guide

To get started on using Ethereum and smart contract development, here is what you need to do:

Step 1:

The first thing you need to do is get a blockchain. Here, you have many options: you can go with geth, parity, pyethapp, or testrpc (the latter is ideal for anyone just seeking a blockchain).

Once you install your preferred blockchain, start with testrpc (this will form a great launching pad for all your development needs).

```
testrpc
```

Once that is in, your blockchain is ready. However, of importance to note is that the above (testrpc) does not mine blocks for ether; -b allows you to specify your preferred block interval—for instance, you can go with 1 second.

Step 2:

The next step in the process is to talk to the blockchain. Once the blockchain is working, download web3.js, install it, open a config.js file, and place this in it.

Here is an illusory image of this:

```
var web3 = require('web3');
var web3_provider = 'http://localhost:8545';
var _web3 = new web3();
_web3.setProvider(new web3.providers.HttpProvider(web3_provider));
exports.web3 = _web3;
```

Once this is up and running, to communicate with the blockchain in your backend server, execute this:

```
var config = require('./config.js');

config.web3.eth.X
```

The X here represents whatever web3 API function you want to, you can find a script for that on GITHUB.

Step 3:

The next step is to write some smart contracts. As a note, however, you will need ether to run the smart contracts. To write smart contracts, you will use solidity. While creating some contracts seems scary and overly technical, it is not, and many applications make the process simple.

You should keep the contracts simple enough because each operation on the Ethereum network costs gas, which means money. Complex smart contracts mean calling your contract can cost you $0.05-$1.50. The second thing is that complex contracts increase the chances of mistakes; since the code that runs the contract is irreversible, keeping the contract simple is best.

The following guide shall show you how to write your first contract in solidity:

http://www.techracers.com/smart-contract-solidity

Step 4:

In step 4, you are going to run/test the smart contract you just created by deploying it. To do so, you will need to use Truffle.

Truffle allows you to manage tester contracts and easily work it into your testing framework. As an example, consider the following package. json script:

```
"scripts": {
  "test": "cd truffle && truffle deploy && truffle test
./myTruffleTest.js && cd .. && npm run myOtherTests"
}
```

This script does three things: its deploys your contract, runs your truffle test, and then runs your regular test. Truffle tests are ideal because they work within the confines of the blockchain technology and deploy into your testing scope different blockchain operations.

To pass the test information to the rest of your test suite, you can use Truffle to save addresses into a configuration file and then import that file into your regular tests. Using web3.js and the configuration file, you can interact with all your contracts in any test.

To deploy your smart contract, go into the truffle directory, and type the following (as this test runs, ensure that testrpc is also running in another window):

```
truffle deploy
```

The following script will print the address of your newly deployed contract. Copy this address into you config.js file or programmatically save it in a truffle test.

Here is an example of the address:

```
exports.contract_addr = '0xe73e8e0a4442e140aea87a4b150ef07b82492500'
```

Step 5:

Next is to make a smart contract call. To call contracts, you can use hex strings or libraries. For this purpose, we shall be using Hex strings.

First, you will need to have everything, number, strings, and the rest in a hex. The other thing is that since Ethereum uses 256 bits words, you will have to left-pad everything that has zeros to 64 characters. The other thing to note is that you will canonically declare types in the function definition. Here is an example.

```
function add(uint x, uint y) public constant returns (uint) {
  return x + y;
}
```

Assume that in the above example, your aim is to add 1 and 2, you will call this function as follows:

First, you would take the first 4 bytes of the keccak 256 hash of your packed canonical function definition. This sounds complex. To make the process easier, head over to this website, type in the function declaration, and then take the first 8 characters. Ethereum uses canonical and shorthand types (for example, uint256 is uint's canonical type). To learn more about the definition and examples of these types, navigate to the following link.

Using the example above, here is how the declaration appears:

```
add(uint256,uint256)
```

This returns the following keccak256 hash:

```
771602f7f25ce61b0d4f2430f7e4789bfd9e6e4029613fda01b7f2c89fbf44ad
```

When we take the first 8 characters (4bytes), we have the following:

```
771602f7
```

Let us pad this to 256 bits parameters:

x=1 is:

```
0000000000000000000000000000000000000000000000000000000000000001
```

y=2 is:

```
0000000000000000000000000000000000000000000000000000000000000002
```

Together, they form:

```
000000000000000000000000000000000000000000000000000000000000010000
0000000000000000000000000000000000000000000000000000000000000002
```

When you pack everything together and add a 0x prefix, we generate the following:

```
0x771602f700000000000000000000000000000000000000000000000000000000000
00001000000000000000000000000000000000000000000000000000000000000000
02
```

With the payload prepared, we can use web3 to call the contract:

```
var config = require('./config.js');

var call =
'0x771602f70000000000000000000000000000000000000000000000000000000000
00000010000000000000000000000000000000000000000000000000000000000000000
002'

var to = config.contract_addr;

var res = config.web3.eth.call({ to: to, data: call });
```

After this, you will get back 3 for res. You will get a BigNumber object as follows:

```
res.toString()
>'3'
```

The following resource details why your DApp development should use BigNumber.

This concludes how to call a contract. The other thing we have to look at is how to write into a contract in instances where you want to change or update it. To do this, you will need to use your private key to sign a contract.

Step 6:

Step 6 involves setting up your account so you can get ether to complete the last statement of step 5 above. For this purpose, you will need to go back into the truffle folder and add the following variable into your config.js file:

NOTE: To execute this step, you will need to get an Ethereum account, which you can get from your private/public keypai. You can use eth-lightwallet for this purpose.

```
var keys = require(`${process.cwd()}/../test/keys.json`);

it('Should send me some ether.', function() {
  assert.notEqual(keys.me.addr, null);

  var eth = 1*Math.pow(10, 18);
  var sendObj = {
    from: accounts[0],
    value: eth,
    to: keys.me.addr
  }

  Promise.resolve(web3.eth.sendTransaction(sendObj))
  .then(function(txHash) {
    assert.notEqual(txHash, null);
    return web3.eth.getBalance(keys.me.addr)
  })
  .then(function(balance) {
    assert.notEqual(balance.toNumber(), 0);
  })
})
```

We are sending 1 ether or 10^18 wei; making transactions or smart contracts calls always uses wei values. Here are the results of this:

```
exports.me = {
  addr: "0x29f2f6405e6a307baded0b0672745691358e3ee6",
  pkey:
"8c2bcfce3d9c4f215fcae9b215eb7c95831da0219ebfe0bb909eb951c3134515"
}
```

As you can see from the above, we are moving ether from accounts [0] that has ether to me.addr housed in your config file.

Step 7:

The next and final step is use your smart contracts to transact. Here, you have three options: the first is to send it to another address as value, the second is to call a contract function — requires that you incentive a miner to process your update (using gas) — and the third and final way is to call a contract that accepts ether as payment to update state.

For our purpose, which, in this example, we are going to have a function that tracks a user's balance, we are going to use the second option. Here is how this looks:

```
function addUserBalance(uint balance)
public returns (bool) {
  if (!accounts[msg.sender]) { throw; }
  if (accounts[msg.sender].balance + balance <
accounts[msg.sender].balance) { throw; }
  accounts[msg.sender].balance += balance;
  return true;
}
```

In the above, the second if statement is necessary because in solidity, adding and subtracting can lead to numerical underflow and overflow—be mindful of this.

Upon calling this function, which we do by sending a transaction, we want to update the global state of the network to reflect the following:

The balance of msg.sender's account has increased. Since those using Ethereum do not have the power to update the state, they need miners and use gas, which translates into ether, to pay for the update services.

Here is how to call this function using Ethereum ABI definition:

```
addUserBalance(uint256) --> 22526328 -->
0x2252632800000000000000000000000000000000000000000000000000000000000000000
1
```

After we have the above data, we can use it to form an unsigned transaction:

```
var data =
'0x225263280000000000000000000000000000000000000000000000000000000000000000
01';
var nonce = config.web3.eth.getTransactionCount(keys.me.addr);
var gasPrice = 20 * Math.pow(10, 9);
var gasLimit = 100000;

var txn = {
  from: config.me.addr,
  to: config.contract_address,
  gas: `0x${gasLimit.toString(16)}`,
  gasPrice: `0x${gasPrice.toString(16)}`,
  data: data,
  nonce: `0x${nonce.toString(16)}`,
  value: '0x0'
}
```

The above cement the need for gas to update the state/make transactions. Gasprice is the amount of wei a miner needs to update the state of your transaction. In an instance where the transaction costs the miner more wei than you provided, the state shall fail to update and the miner shall still keep all the gas money provided with the transaction. If the wei you provided is above what the miner needs to update the state, he or she will refund the remainder.

If we send the following to the network, the state shall fail to update because this instance lacks proof of who is authorizing the transaction. To make sure the transaction updates (assuming we have enough gas money), we need to our private key to sign the transaction. This key is in your private file (refer to steps 1 through 4). Here is what you need to do with the key stored in your config file.

```
var Tx = require('ethereumjs-tx');

var privateKey = Buffer.from(config.me.pkey, 'hex')
var tx = new Tx(txn);
tx.sign(privateKey);
var serializedTx = tx.serialize();
```

In the above, we are using libraries to use the private key to sign a transaction. The following should return this:

```
0xf8aa808504a817c800830f424094a0f68379088f9aee95ba5c9d178693b874c4cd6880b
844a9059cbb0000000000000000000000000053b2188b0b100e68299708864e2ccecb62cdf
0d0000000000000000000000000000000000000000000000000000000746a5288001ca01f6
83f083c2d7c741a1218efc0144adc1749125a9ca53134b06353a8e4ef72afa07c50fb5964
7ff8b8895b75795b0f51de745fa5987b985f7d1025eb346755bca0
```

We can then use web3 to submit this to the blockchain, which upon doing so, will return a transaction hash, which simply put, is not proof of a successful transaction but a hash of the provided transaction.

```
var txHash = config.web3.eth.sendRawTransaction(raw_txn);
```

Which will look as follows:

```
0xac8914ecb06b333a9e655a85a0cd0cccddb8ac627098e7c40877d27a130a7293
```

The last step is to confirm that the transaction has processed successfully: get the transacton receipt. Here is how to do that:

```
var txReceipt = config.web3.eth.getTransactionReceipt(txHash);
```

If the above returns null, the transaction was unsuccessful. There are various reasons for this: perhaps you failed to include enough wei, or perhaps you used the wrong private key to sign the file.

That is how to get started on using blockchain and smart contract development. As you so obviously noted, this process is very technical. To avoid feeling overwhelmed, go through each of the steps gradually until you comprehend how to do this and whenever you feel lost, use this section as a reference guide. In addition, be comfortable with spending a substantial amount of time on this process because, to get it, you will need to go back to the step several times and read the documentations attached. Once you master everything we have discussed in this subsection, you will be well on your way to being a capable Ethereum developer.

Now that we have hashed out how to start using blockchain, let us now discuss cryptocurrencies, the technology that is driving the uptake and use of blockchain, and changing how we use money today and in the future.

Section 5: The Future of Money: A Cryptocurrencies et al Guide for Beginners

Cryptocurrencies is the new buzzword. Banks, prominent software and accounting firms, and even brick and motor businesses, are openly accepting it. Many are trading cryptocurrencies such as bitcoin and in the process enriching themselves. Unfortunately, even though cryptocurrencies are popular, they have become a sort of 21st century unicorn in that very few people actually know what they are. In this section of the guide, we are going to demystify cryptocurrencies by stripping them to their bare minimum.

Understanding Cryptocurrencies and their Emergence

Cryptocurrencies are digital assets used as a medium of exchange and designed to use cryptography to secure transactions and control the creation of new units of the currency. Cryptocurrencies are virtual currencies or digital currencies.

They (cryptocurrencies) use cryptography and shared ledger (on the blockchain platform) to create a stable, secure, traceable, and open-source monetary system. The name cryptocurrency comes from the fact that they use cryptographic code. Cryptography is a way to encrypt and secure information with the intent to ensure that as a network sends this information, it is secure in that unauthorized persons cannot access the information.

Before 2008, which is when the first cryptocurrency hit mainstream use, many had tried their hand at developing a decentralized and cryptography-secured currency that used distributed networks. The launch of Bitcoin in 2008-09 changed all this, which is perhaps why to date Bitcoins are still the most popular and widely used cryptocurrency despite there being various other cryptocurrencies such as Litecoin, Ripple, and Dogecoin.

What most people do not know is that the development of cryptocurrencies came about as a side effect of another invention. In his 2008 white paper, Satoshi says he created "a peer-to-peer electric payment/cash system." His innovation created a decentralized digital cash system, something many before him had tried and failed to do.

His decision to create this system of payment led to the birth of cryptocurrencies and, as Satoshi says in an email to Dustin Trammel, a Bitcoin pioneer user, cryptocurrencies proved the missing link in the creation of decentralized digital cash.

Digital cash works as follows: to maintain a properly working digital cash system, you need three things - accounts, balances, and transactions. As we discussed earlier, a key problem digital cash systems run into is the problem of double spending: making sure users cannot spend money more than once. In a normal digital cash system, the system uses a central server as the repository for records of balances.

The decentralized digital cash payment system Satoshi created eliminated the need for a central server and, instead, used a peer-to-peer model where every node (computer) on the network played a role in the processing of records. In this system, every computer on the peer network keeps a history of all transactions and checks that all transactions are valid and by so doing, helps avoid the problem of double spending. To achieve this, the computers on the network have to achieve consensus.

Stripped down to its barest minimum, cryptocurrencies are entries in a public ledger no one can change at will, and in instances where someone has to change the entries, he or she has to fulfil specific pre-set conditions.

To quantify this, consider the money you have in your fiat currency bank account; such monies are nothing more than entries in a database that can only change when you meet specific conditions. For instance, when you withdraw a specific amount of money from your bank account, if you have insufficient funds, the transaction shall fail to process because the command fails to meet specific conditions. In this case, the condition is sufficient balance. Money, in any form, is nothing but entries in a database that has three main criteria: accounts, balance, and transactions.

How Cryptocurrencies Work

At this point in the book, you know much about how cryptocurrencies work because, in essence, they use the working modalities of the blockchain network.

For specificity, a blockchain-based cryptocurrency such as Bitcoin operates on the premise of a peer network. Each of the nodes (computers) on the network has a complete historical record of every transaction in its history and thus, it has the history of the balance in each account or wallet. Simplified, a transaction is file a file saying X gives Y Z amounts of Bitcoins and uses his private key to sign this file, thereby making it authentic. After X signs the file, the file transmits to the network from one peer to the other, leaving a history of the transactions.

Since cryptocurrencies are decentralized, rather than being in the control of financial institutions or governments, they use math, and while they are similar to fiat currencies in that their value appreciates and depreciates against fiat currencies, their scarcity depends on math instead of centralized monetary policies or the influence from one group or the other.

Their value does not depend on the availability of gold or other physical goods, and governments cannot create them as they would normal currencies. The above is because, as we have stated, cryptocurrencies use a P2P (peer-to-peer) transactional systems independent from third parties.

Since they ride upon the blockchain, to ensure the legitimacy of each transaction, they use complex mathematical puzzles/equations to link accounts with amount of digital currency an account holder would like to transact. Similar to the blockchain technology—they use the same technology after all—the system uses the computing power of miners to solve these equations and in return, the miners get a portion of the cryptocurrency.

Here is an illustration of how miners create new coins and confirm transactions within the cryptocurrency network:

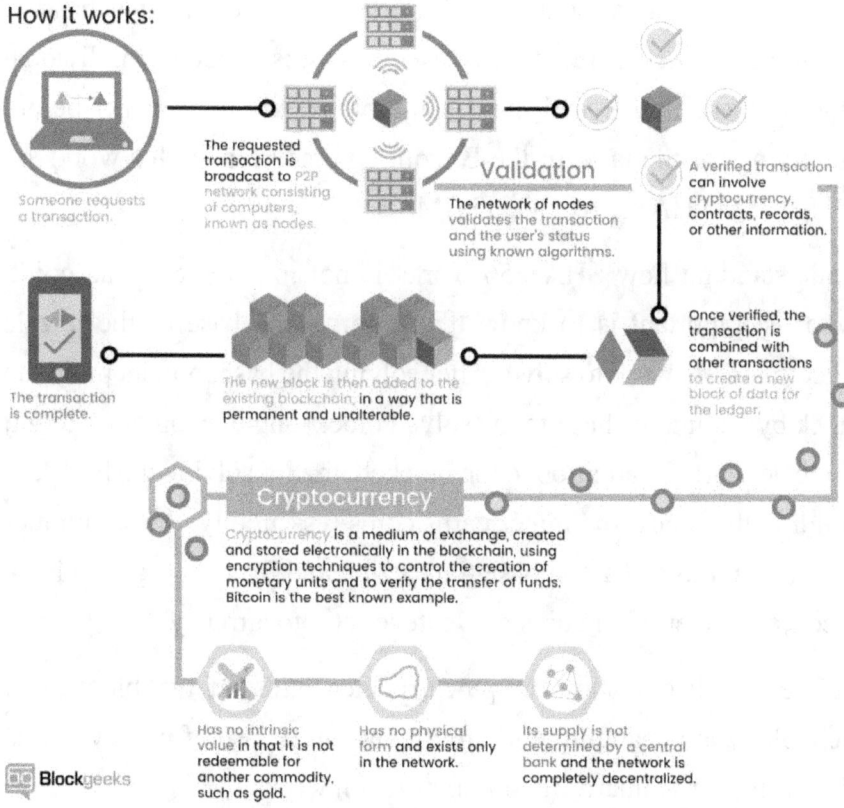

Image courtesy of Blockgeeks.com

Since a decentralized network lacks an authority who decides who should do what, anyone with computing power can become a miner. Clearly, this presents a problem because those with higher computing power would dominate the network, thereby becoming authorities, which would defeat the purpose of decentralization (we talked about this earlier). This means each cryptocurrency network must have in place a mechanism that keeps those with superior computing power from ruling the network.

To overcome this hurdle, Satoshi created a rule stating that miners have to invest a fair amount of work (what we called a hash, a cryptographic key or function whose purpose is to connect individual blocks to each other and then to the block: proof of work) before qualifying for the task. In the Bitcoin cryptocurrency, this works on the SHA 256 HASH ALGORITHM.

Understanding how SHA 256 works is not important at this point. What is important is to know that it forms the base of the puzzle Bitcoin miners work to solve. After solving the hash, miners build the block by adding the hash to the solved block, and then broadcasting it to the network for addition to the blockchain. For solving the hash and building the block, the miner earns coins (essentially, the said miner has the right to add a coinbase transaction and by so doing, receive a specific number of Bitcoins or whatever cryptocurrency).

Before we discuss how cryptocurrencies built on the blockchain technology are changing our current and future use of money, let us discuss how a standard Bitcoin transaction works.

Bitcoin Lifecycle: How Cryptocurrency Transactions Work

Since Bitcoins are the most popular forms of cryptocurrencies, this subsection shall concentrate on detailing how a Bitcoin transaction works.

The use and transference of Bitcoins (and other cryptocurrencies) requires a Wallet. What most people do not realize is that, contrary to popular belief, Bitcoins exist nowhere (they are in fact, nonexistent) and instead, what we have are records of Bitcoin transactions between different Bitcoin addresses. The transactions as recorded have increasing and decreasing balances; the only way to work out the balance within a certain Bitcoin address would be to recreate the blockchain, which would take immense computing power and work.

Transactions within the bitcoin system have three key elements: (1) the input, this records the origin of the transaction (the Bitcoin address), (2) the amount of Bitcoin transacted, and (3) the recipients Bitcoin address (called the output).

To send or receive Bitcoins, you need two things: an address (a bitcoin address) and a private key. As discussed earlier, the Bitcoin address is a series of random numbers and letters. The easiest way to get a Bitcoin address is to sign up for a Bitcoin wallet. Some of the best options include Bitcoin Wallet, CoPay, and the other wallets listed on this site. The private key also comes with the wallet, but unlike the Bitcoin address that you can share with those you are asking payment from, the private key is exactly that, private, and as such, you should not share it with anyone.

When sending bitcoins to someone, which means you are sending the person an encrypted file, you use the private key to sign the file. If you fail to use a key or the key you use is incorrect, the transaction shall fail. Wallets have made the idea of sending Bitcoins easy; all you have to do is log into the wallet, select the send option, enter an amount, sign the file, and then send it out to the network where if the transaction has enough transactional fees, miners will verify the transaction, and place it into the ledger. A combination of transactions makes up the cryptographic puzzle that, when solved, leads to the creation of new blockchains and additional currencies. This is how Bitcoin transactions work.

The following like has an invaluable infographic on the lifecycle of a Bitcoin transaction.

http://bitcoinfographics.com/en/transaction-life-cycle/

As we have discussed, and as this book has shown you, blockchain based technologies and monies will be an integral part of our future. This means that to make sure you are ready for the future, you have to learn as much as you can about these currencies. This book has done a fair job of teaching you this.

To complete the knowledge in this book, we shall close the book by discussing how to start investing in cryptocurrencies (which currencies to invest in) and how to invest in blockchain.

How to Invest In Blockchain and Cryptocurrencies

The rapid uptake of blockchain-based technologies such as Bitcoin means these technologies will shape our future in many ways. This also means that the best time to invest in them is now. As an example, in early March 2017, 1 BTC was worth $1,000. In August, the same traded at $4,400 to the dollar; this means the value appreciated by over $3,000.

As a note however, investing in cryptocurrencies is different from investing in stock in that its takes a different form. Investing in a company means you are buying the shares of that company, which also means you own part of that company. When you invest in cryptocurrencies, you invest in something different: when you invest in Bitcoins, you buy the virtual currency; when you invest in Ethereum, you get gas, the power that runs smart contracts and decentralized apps, and that translates into Ether, the Ethereum cryptocurrecy.

To trade cryptocurrencies, you have to create an account with one of the various dedicated exchanges, such as Kraken, GDAX, and Geminin. These exchanges allow you to use fiat currencies to buy bitcoins and then change them into fiat currencies when you sell your Bitcoins. The best cryptocurrencies to invest include Bitcoins, Ethereum, Litecoin, Monero, Bitcoin Cash, Ripple, and Zcash.

On the other hand, as we have discussed, blockchain is the technology that cryptocurrencies ride upon; you can invest in blockchain without directing your money into buying cryptocurrencies. For instance, you can invest in blockchain-based startups. You can find some of these startups on crowdfunding platforms such as BNKToTheFuture. Another way to invest in these startups is by investing ICOs (initial coin offerings) of new blockchain technologies. Companies developing blockchain-based technologies often issue tokens or cryptocurrencies as a way to raise development capital. While this form of investment is risky, the returns are stellar.

If you would like to invest in blockchain-based companies, the best options are BTCS, Global Arena Holding, DigitalX, BTL Group, Coinsilium Group, and First Bitcoin Capital.

Obviously, investing in these new technologies will require due prudence. Do not get into a trading a specific cryptocurrecny or invest into a specific blockchain startup if you are not sure of what you are doing; that is a recipe for failure and massive losses. Further, if you buy Bitcoins (and other cryptocurrencies) low, hold them — do not be a day trader who trades when the value moves a mere few points). As you saw earlier, in the span of 3 or so months, the value of Bitcoin jumped from below $1,000 to over $4,400. This essentially means that investing in these technologies is not for the faint hearted or those in for quick profits.

Conclusion

This guide has given you every bit of information you could ever want on the history of money, the blockchain, cryptocurrencies, and throughout this discussion, you glimpsed what the future holds for us. Use this information to educate yourself and others. If you feel so compelled, invest in this technology because, if evidence is anything to go by, blockchain-based technologies will change our daily lives more in how we view, use, and even store money.

Part 2: Bitcoin

An Essential Beginner's Guide to Bitcoin Investing, Mining and Cryptocurrency Technologies

Introduction

This book has comprehensive beginner-friendly information about bitcoin investing, mining and cryptocurrency technologies.

Bitcoin and cryptocurrencies are taking over the world by storm. Think about it; bitcoin started less 10 years ago and today, it is perhaps the world's most valuable currency (even if not widely accepted) with one bitcoin selling at over $10 000! Very few things can record such a massive price increase within such a short period. And the good thing about bitcoins is that you don't have to do anything once you have them; all you should do is to sit back and wait for prices to rise! You could even make money verifying and validating transactions in what's referred to as mining.

Would you like to just sit back and watch your money multiply? Then investing and trading in cryptocurrencies might be all you need if we were to look at 2017 as an example. Bitcoin is one of these cryptocurrencies that you can use to grow and diversify your investment portfolio, as it is increasingly becoming a powerful form of currency due to its reliance on the immutable decentralized technology as well as its revolutionary ingenuity to operate without middlemen or any other central authority.

This guide is meant to help you understand the basics of investing in bitcoin, so you can learn how to benefit from its unique features while carefully guarding yourself against any forthcoming online risks. In the end, you'll gather enough confidence and start taking advantage of this entirely new market while being conscious of its future.

Hopefully, bitcoin's nature and relentless increasing value will fascinate you more and inspire you to make more money. However, always remember that hard work pays; a bit of toil will see you reap more.

Understanding Cryptocurrency: An Introduction To Cryptocurrency & The Simplest Explanation Of Bitcoin And Cryptocurrency That You Will Ever Read

An Introduction To Cryptocurrency

The one thing that most cryptocurrency investors do wrong is they go straight to the investment part, whether they are reading up on the subject or actually doing the investment itself, without making sure they have enough base information to help them on their journey. This chapter is here so that you do not make the same mistake.

What Is Cryptocurrency?

Simply put, a cryptocurrency is a token in digital form that is designed to work as an exchange medium or as a method of record keeping. It uses cryptographic algorithms to secure as well as verify the transactions across its network and to have in control, the creations of new tokens.

Bitcoin is a form of cryptocurrency i.e. a form of decentralized digital currency (under the category of cryptocurrencies) that is created and held electronically. Unlike other currencies, which are issued by the government, bitcoin works without any central repository or a single administrator. Instead, it operates on a cryptography technology to secure various transactions as well as control the creation of additional units and verify the transfer of various assets.

How Does Bitcoin, And By Extension, Most Cryptocurrencies Work?

Bitcoin employs peer-to-peer transactions where there is no financial institution or middleman involved. The records of each transaction are verified cryptographically by other "nodes" on the network. What follows is that those transactions are combined into a "block" and added to the cryptocurrency's ledger. This is otherwise known as the "blockchain".

The blockchain will hold details of every single transaction on the network, and as this blockchain is simultaneously held on several nodes throughout the blockchain network, it is impossible to change, censor, hack or disrupt it in any way. The nodes on the network, referred to as "miners", will collect a small fee from each transaction. This fee works as an incentive for having the network available online.

The Follow-The-Leader Effect Of Bitcoin:

The release of Bitcoin in 2009 opened the door for hundreds of new cryptocurrencies to be created and introduced into the market. They all tend to serve their own individual purpose. After Bitcoin, Ethereum is the most successful platform.

Ethereum allows you to attach "smart contracts" to your transactions, which execute without the possibility of censorship, downtime, fraud or 3rd party interference. Almost every other cryptocurrency created has either borrowed the Bitcoin concept or the Ethereum one. What the creators do is that they seek to improve on them and the features added to their code-bases.

Some of the 'alt-coins" are more privacy-oriented more than anything else while others largely ignore this quality and focus wholly on transaction speed. More commonly these days, a lot of the coins that are being released are launched to fund projects, rather than the project-owner having to seek venture capital.

The Simplest Explanation for Bitcoin and Cryptocurrency That You Will Ever Read

You may be reading this book because Bitcoin, or some other cryptocurrency, has piqued your interest to the point where you just had to learn more about it. Even more so, you may be here because you have had a tough time of understanding how cryptocurrency works. It could even be that the 1st part of this chapter has done little to help you understand cryptocurrency. You want to get into the game, but how can you do it if your knowledge of it is scarce? Is Bitcoin valid? Can you trust the digital system? It is one thing for somebody to hand you some cash- as long as it is in your hands, it is yours and it is in nobody else's hands. But is digital currency this straightforward? Can copies of it be made? You may have a million of such questions nagging you. By the end of this chapter, you will have them no longer.

This chapter will call for some basic imagination; nothing too fancy however.

The apple

You and I are sitting on a park bench, with some larks singing about us. It is a lovely day. I have one apple in my hand. I stretch my arm and give you that apple. You now have my apple and as a consequence, I have no apples. This was very simple, was it not?

Let us examine exactly what happened:

I put my apple physically in your hand. You and I know it happened, as we were both there. You touched the apple; perhaps waited until I had left so that you could eat it all by yourself. You can remember how it tasted. All of this is sufficient proof that I gave you my apple. We did not need a 3rd party present to help us make the transfer possible.

Can I give you an apple now? Sure I could, but it would have to be another apple. I cannot give you the same apple since I already gave it to you the first time. I have no control over that apple anymore, as it left my possession completely. Assuming you do not eat it, you can give it to your friend if you so fancy, and then your friend can give it to another friend and so on.

This is what an in-person exchange that involves conventional goods looks like. It really is the same whether I choose to give you a banana instead or choose to keep my fruits and give you a $5 bill or maybe a book on how to graft apples.

The "digital" apple

Let us say I have one digital apple on my person, and I want to give to you. Here you go, have this digital apple and do with it what you want. But it is hard to deny that unlike our first scenario with the physical apple, things get very interesting here.

How can you tell that digital apple which used to be in my possession is now yours and only yours? Think about this for a second. This is surely more complicated, right? How can you tell that I did not send it to my uncle John as an e-mail attachment before I gave it to you, or your friend Lisa?

Perhaps, I made three copies of that digital apple on my laptop computer to keep for myself. Maybe I put it up on my blog and all my 32,400 subscribers had a chance to download it for free.

As you can see, digital exchange presents some problems. Sending digital items is not really the same thing as sending physical ones. Some software scientists have even come up with a name for this problem- "double spending problem". However, you do not need to worry anymore. Let us try to think up a solution here, and work our way up to the Bitcoin system.

The ledger

Perhaps, the thing to do is to have these digital apples tracked in a ledger. A ledger is basically a book that you use to track every transaction. It is an accounting book for transaction records.

Our ledger, since it is a digital one, needs to live in the digital world and have a person who understands this world in charge of it. This is just like World of Warcraft, the game. The game's development company, Blizzard, has a "digital ledger" of every sword and stick in their system. It is thus possible to have someone like them track our digital apples, right? We've finally made progress and solved our problem!

More problems

We are not completely in the clear, however. We have a bit of a problem in our hands:

1. What if some other fellow at Blizzard created his own stash of digital apples secretly? He could just dip into his illegal collection and add them in to balance things whenever he feels like it.

2. It is not quite the same way it was when you and I sat on the park bench that day and I handed you my apple. Going through our digital ledger tracking party, in our hypothetical case Blizzard, is like setting up a courthouse, with all of the court's rules- such as the "you are innocent until proven guilty" kind that have seen murderers walk scot free- and tossing out the judge and jury. Basically, what you have is a jungle- a civilized jungle, but a jungle just the same.

How Can I Just Hand Over The Digital Apple To You In The Usual Manner?

Is there any way we can really replicate our transaction digitally so it resembles our park bench situation?

The remedy

What if we gave this ledger to each and everybody? Instead of this ledger living in the Blizzard computer and being unavailable to other parties, it will stay in the computers of everybody. Every transaction of digital apples that happens, including our own, will be recorded in this ledger that everybody has.

It is impossible to cheat it- how can I send you digital apples I do not possess knowing full well that it would not synchronize with all the other parties in the system? It is an incredibly tough system to beat. It would be even harder to beat if it got big. If it got global, then it would truly be impossible beat.

In addition, it is not controlled by just one person. Thus, I know that even if I wanted to cheat the system and add digital apples to my account that I do not have, I cannot do it as my efforts would be worthless. The rules of the system, which were defined at the very beginning, will ensure this is so.

What is more, the rules and code are open source- a bit like the software that you use in your Android phone. Anybody can access and download it on Google Play store. You can also think of the rules and code being like Wikipedia- it is there for smart people to secure, maintain, improve upon it and check on it every so often.

If you so wanted, you could participate in this network as well. You could be involved in updating this ledger and making sure that everything checks out. It is not difficult to be motivated to do so, especially if you are invested in the system. For your trouble, you could get, say, 24 apples as a reward. In fact, this is the only way to create more apples in the system. This is what cryptocurrency enthusiasts refer to as mining. Otherwise, you just have to look for somebody who is willing to sell you some digital ones.

Note that this is a really simplified analogy. However, nothing has been passed over- this is exactly how the system works, and it is indeed a real system in place. In Bitcoin, it is referred to as the Bitcoin protocol. You see all those digital apples we have been talking about? These are the Bitcoin, or other cryptocurrency that you may fancy getting into.

What does the public ledger allow for?

1. It is an open source, as you may recall. The total number of digital apples, or Bitcoin, was defined in the public ledger at the very beginning. You and I both know the exact amount in existence. Within this system, we know that these digital apples are limited and that the total number will not change.

2. When we trade and I hand over the digital apple, or Bitcoin, to you, I now know that the digital apple left my possession certifiably. The ledger in everybody's computer will confirm as much, as the transaction information will be updated and verified by the ledger.

3. Since the ledger is public owned, I did not need my Uncle John, who worked as a judge sometime in his life, to make sure I did not cheat or manufacture some extra copies to keep for myself. With regard to Bitcoin, I do not need the bank or the government to put their stamp of validity on our transaction. The 3rd party has no use.

Thus, within this system, the exchange of the digital apple is now just like that of a physical one. It is now as straightforward as seeing a physical apple leave my hand and get into yours. Just as was the case in the park bench, the exchange only involved you and I. We did not need my uncle John, or the bank/government, to certify its validity.

To put it in fewer words, it now behaves like a physical object would and yet, it is still as digital as ever. We can deal 1000 apples, if we fancied it, provided I had the apples in my possession and you had enough to trade for them. We could even make them a million digital apples or 0.001 apples, as long as the math checks out. I can send you the apple with just one click of a button, and I could put it in your digital pocket, or wallet, even if I was in Somalia and you were in Washington DC.

This is exactly how cryptocurrency, Bitcoin being the clear leader here, works.

Let's take the discussion a bit further.

Definition of Terms

This chapter builds on the previous one, and is vital in that it will help you better understand the rest of the contents of this book. You see, a lot of terms get thrown around, and if you are new to cryptocurrency, it can all get quite confusing. This chapter will help you understand the various cryptocurrency terms and even more importantly, the context in which they are used.

Without further ado, let's understand some terms used in cryptocurrencies.

Note: For illustration purposes, we will use a conversation between two people to help you understand the context in which different terms can be used.

Cryptocurrency

This "is a digital asset that is designed to work as an exchange medium, using cryptography to secure transactions as well as to control the creation of additional units of this currency."

Examples: Bitcoin, Ethereum, Dogecoin and multiple other altcoins

Illustration:

Kevin: "Joe, my good friend, I have been trading cryptocurrency for a while now. It's great for some good side money."

Joe: "What do you mean by cryptocurrency, Kevin? What is that? Do you maybe mean forex?

Kevin: "No Joe, I mean Bitcoin and other altcoins."

Address

This can be described as a code to send, store and receive Bitcoin and other crypto currency. It consists of anywhere between 26 and 35 characters. You could also say that it is the public key used by holders of cryptocurrency to sign transactions digitally.

Example of an address:

175tWpbnb8K1S7NmmsH4Zx6rkiewF9WQrcZv245W

Illustration:

Kevin: "Say, Joe, what is your address so I can send you a few Bitcoin?

Joe: "It is 93 Almeria Street."

Kevin: "No Joe, come on! I am not asking for your home address. I mean your Bitcoin one! And by the way, make sure you give me the accurate address or your coins will get lost!"

Joe: Oh, my bad. It is

175tWpbnb8K1S7NmmsH4Zx6rkiewF9WQrcZv245W

Altcoin

This is the community-accepted name for any coin that is not bitcoin. Altcoins include Ethereum, Monero, Dodgecoin and Dash.

Example: Steem, Litecoin, Ethereum and Dogecoin.

Illustration:

Kevin: Joe, did you manage to buy some good altcoins?

Joe: Oh, I actually did, Bob! I bought some Litecoin, a few Dogecoin and lots of POTcoin! I'm telling you, I was on a roll today.

Block

These are essentially pages in a record keeping book or ledger. Blocks are those files where data that cannot be altered, which is related to the network, gets permanently stored. Since this data cannot be deleted or disrupted in any way, it will be around forever.

Blockchain

This is basically a full list of all the blocks which have been mined since Bitcoin, or other relevant cryptocurrency, was created.

Block reward

This refers to the reward you get for hashing i.e. solving the mathematical equation, which is related to a particular block. For example, 25 bitcoins are awarded for every block mined. This usually halves for every 210,000 blocks.

Illustration:

Kevin: "I am making almost $3 in a day mining Dogecoin and Litecoin!"

Joe: "Brother, you need to upgrade your mining contracts. I am making at least 15 times that amount on Ethereum!"

Mining difficulty

This term points to a number. This number will determine just how difficult it is to hash a new block. It is relative to the maximum number allowed in a certain numerical portion of a block's hash. The lower this number is, the more difficult it becomes to produce a hash value fitting it.

Hash

This is a mathematical process, which takes a variable data amount and produces shorter, fixed length outputs.

DDoS

This is a "Distributed Denial of Service" attack. It uses a large number of computers, which the attacker has in his control, to drain the resources of a centralized target.

Joe: "Hey, Kevin! I cannot get my coins off of Coinbase and the value is dipping pretty fast!"

Kevin: "That is most likely because some fellow is DDoS'ing it. Joe, this is why it is vital that you store your coins in a safe and secure wallet."

Dust transaction

This refers to a transaction that involves a very small Bitcoin amount, which offers low financial value but takes up space in the blockchain just the same.

Example: A "Satoshi" worth of Bitcoin

Illustration:

Joe: "Kevin, Bitcoin is way too expensive to purchase!"

Kevin: "You do not have to purchase a whole Bitcoin my man. Just purchase a few "Satoshis" worth of it.

Escrow

This is the act of holding assets or funds in a 3rd party account so as to protect them in the event of an anonymous transaction.

Fiat

This refers to any form of regulated and centralized physical paper money.

Illustration:

Kevin: "Joe, I am hoping you have been trading your fiat for Bitcoin."

Joe: "Kevin, I would rather hang myself than drive a Fiat."

Kevin: "You are a funny guy, Joe. I meant Fiat currency, not Fiat the car model."

FOMO

This stands for "Fear of Missing Out." You may have been compelled by FOMO, for instance, to seek out this book and read it, which is a good thing.

FUD

"Fear, Uncertainty, Doubt."

Hardfork

This is a permanent divergence of an alternative operating vision, of the current blockchain. Forks will come into place when a bug in the program occurs or more commonly, a new set of rules come into play.

These will happen when a team of developers creates and then inserts changes that are notably substantial in the system.

Simply put, this is an alteration to the Bitcoin or other cryptocurrency block structure, which has an effect on the difficulty rules.

ICO

This is an "Initial Coin Offering." This is often used as a way for new cryptocurrency projects to raise money for the project by offering a certain amount of coins for sale to the people at the base price.

Illustration:

Joe: "Say Kevin, why is my BNT token worth a lot less than what I purchased it for in ICO?"

Kevin: "Joe, you made the mistake of buying into that hype. Never make the mistake of buying into that hype."

Mining

This is the action of generating new Bitcoin by solving cryptographic problems via computing hardware.

Pump and Dump

This refers to exaggerating the value of a given financial asset that may have either been acquired or produced cheaply via aggressive publicity and statements that are mostly misleading.

Illustration:

Joe: "I say Kevin, Parkbyte is shooting for the moon! Purchase it ASAP!"

Kevin: "Joe, this is what we call a pump and dump. It's all nonsense. I would stay away if I were you."

Proof of Work

This is a system that ties your mining capability to your power of computation.

Proof of Stake

This system uses your existing stake to calculate the currency amount that you are able to mine.

Shorting

This is the act of selling cryptocurrency in the hopes of buying it back at a cheaper price and making a profit.

Illustration:

Joe: "Kevin, I just shorted my Bitcoin at $2700. I will be swimming in cash when it dips to $2000, as it is bound to do soon."

Kevin: "Oh Joe, what an immense fool you are. Have you checked the prices just now? It shot to $10,000! I am a rich man!"

Wallet

This is a physical or digital address where cryptocurrency may be sent, stored or received. It is accessible using a private key.

Whale

This is somebody who is in possession of a majority percentage of a cryptocurrency.

A good example of a couple of whales is the Winklevoss twins.

Next up is coverage on blockchain technology; the platform upon which cryptocurrencies operate and credit their validity to.

Blockchain Technology

You will come across the term "blockchain" more than a few times as far as cryptocurrency goes, both in this book and in any other source of information you read. It is thus important that you understand what blockchain technology is and how it works. Here, you will get to understand what blockchain technology is all about as well as the rules that govern it.

What Is A Blockchain?

This is a decentralized, digitized, public ledger of every cryptocurrency transaction. A blockchain is constantly growing as more and more 'solved' blocks are chronologically recorded and added to the chain. This allows the participants of the market to monitor the currency transactions without the need for a central method of record keeping (think of the situation you have in banks, for instance). Remember our apple analogy in Chapter 1, and having the public keep track of digital apples?

Each node, which is to say each computer that is part of the system, automatically downloads gets a copy of the entire blockchain. The blockchain constitutes our ledger.

Dissecting the "Blockchain"

A "block" is the current blockchain 'part'. It records some or all of the most recent transactions. Once this is completed, a new block gets generated. A blockchain has an infinite number of blocks that are connected to each other, in the same way various links are usually connected on a chain, in proper linear, chronological order.

Each block has a hash of the previous block. The blockchain will have complete information about different addresses of users and their balances starting from the genesis block up to the latest one.

The blockchain was designed so that the transactions cannot be deleted. In fact, the blocks get added via cryptography, making sure that they stay in a change-proof condition. The data may be distributed but it cannot be copied.

Bitcoin and blockchains

The blockchain is, unarguably, the major tech innovation of Bitcoin. As has been mentioned several times already, Bitcoin is not subject to regulation by a centralized authority. Rather, the Bitcoin users dictate and validate transactions when one party pays another party for goods and services, effectively eliminating the need for a 3rd party to process and store payments. The completed transaction is recorded publicly into blocks and ultimately into the blockchain. Here, it is verified and then relayed by other users of Bitcoin. On average, a new block is appended to the blockchain approximately every 10 minutes, via mining.

Blockchain extensions in the real world

Let me use an example of what happens in banking to explain this. You can think of the blockchain as a full history of the financial transactions of a financial institution. Each block is like an individual bank statement. But since it is a distributed database system that serves as an open electronic ledger, a blockchain vastly simplifies business operations for all parties. For these very reasons, this technology has become very attractive not only to stock exchanges and financial institutions but to many other fields that are removed from the financial scene, such as music. Advocates have also suggested that this kind of electronic logging system may be very useful if applied to voting systems; vehicle and weapon registration by governments, medical records and even in the confirmation of the ownership of valuables like antiquities.

Comparison between Digital Currency & Fiat Currency

The next step is to compare digital and fiat currencies. How does digital currency compare with fiat (traditional) currency? Other than the obvious knowledge of digital currency having only exchange value (which means it only has value when somebody else is willing to pay for it and thus, no use value), what are the sapient traits of a digital currency like Bitcoin and how does it hold up to traditional currency?

Digital currency, unlike fiat currency, is not bound to any institution or country

In so many ways, digital currency like Bitcoin is very much like traditional currency. It has value, may be used to purchase things and its value is reliant to changes in various market variables. For example, the recent rapid increases in demand for bitcoin in the past year has seen its price increase to a record high of $9,000!

However, unlike traditional currency, digital currency is not bound to any institution or country. As such, it is not subject to authorities like banks and governments, and they have no control over it.

Digital currency is based around total simplicity, an ideal fiat currencies seem to be running away from

It may not look like it at first, especially due to the technological foundation of digital currencies, but they are based around a very simple ideal- people from all parts of the world; from any country or class; should be able to exchange products, credits and services freely, easily and instantly; without needing any intermediary bodies such as banks, payment gateways and merchant accounts. In this way, it really is a transformation to a purer form of trade where you traded what you had when you could, without so many walls in between.

You may be asking yourself, "But does not the tech based platform and reliance on the internet complicate this simplicity? Think of this though; how else would such global reach be achieved if the internet and technology were out of the equation? The internet is the simplest and most practical platform available.

Digital currency has parallels with gold, something fiat currency cannot boast of

With gold, the more you mine it, the less of it there is and as a result, the higher its value rises. The unchangeable principles that govern Bitcoin are similar. Bitcoin technology can only ever produce a certain amount of Bitcoin. Thus, the more Bitcoins that get produced, the harder it becomes to create new ones. This is why we say "mining Bitcoin". Fiat money on the other hand does not have such clear-cut principles governing it, which is why governments are able to just keep printing more and more of it, inevitably leading to plummeting value.

After getting familiarized with bitcoin, now you can start investing in bitcoin. This is the only opportunity you get to test what you have gathered so far. So, in the next chapter, we are delving in the twists and turns of investing in bitcoin and help you get started with your investment.

Investing In Bitcoin

This guide recognizes that bitcoin remains to be one of the many trendy cryptocurrencies that you can choose as your investment vehicle. It is important to note that bitcoin possesses a great potential of actualizing the many 'rags to riches' fairy tales, but it remains unpredictable, mainly due to its volatility. So, as a beginner, it is prudent to consider investing only that amount of money that you are ready to risk losing.

Remember, as your grow older, your financial responsibilities increase. Therefore, the following guidelines will help you to avoid going through any emotional torment, just in case your investment in bitcoin doesn't work as anticipated:

- If you're aged over 40 years, then direct 10% of your investments to bitcoin, while 70% should still go to traditional forms of investment.

- If you're aged between 30 and 40 years, then consider investing 20% in bitcoin while the other traditional investment methods take the remaining 60%.

- But if you're less than 30 years old, then letting up to 30% of your investments be in form of bitcoin won't be a bad idea.

The above guidelines aren't as binding as such. You can just diversify your coins as much as you can, depending on your level of risk tolerance.

With that in mind, let's get started with bitcoin investment.

Getting Started

Getting started with bitcoin is quite easy, even for a novice. Just download the application or use the web application in order to start trading with bitcoin. Once you log into the bitcoin network, you find 3 major applications of the bitcoin client software. If you're keen enough, you will also notice that another implementation exists, which is referred to as the "Satoshi Client" or a "reference implementation." The Satoshi Client is derived from the original application authored by Satoshi Nakamoto and is normally managed by a team of developers as an open source project.

Below are the three major forms of clients that you'll find on the bitcoin network:

- A web client: You can access a web client through a web browser. The most striking feature of this implementation is that you'll have to store your wallet on a server that's owned and controlled by a third party. A web client operates in a manner similar to your webmail, because it depends fully on a server from a third party.

- Light client: With this implementation, you will get an opportunity to store your wallet though you will still rely on a server owned by a third party in order to get access to the network and the bitcoin transactions. The light client doesn't store a full copy of all transactions. And that's where third party servers come in handy, since they carry out the entire validation process of all transactions. You could compare this to a standalone email client that must be connected to a mail server in order to access the mailbox. In this case, the light client depends on a third party in order to interact with the network.

- Full client: This is also called a full node. If you are such a client, you can store the full history of the bitcoin transactions and initiate transactions directly on the bitcoin network while managing your wallets. This operates in the same way as a standalone email server because it has the potential to undertake all aspects of the protocol without any assistance from third party services or other servers.

Your choice of the bitcoin client will solely depend on the amount of control you want over your funds. Operating a full client account will give the highest level of independence and control. However, you'll have to come up with effective mechanisms to back up your transactions and secure your funds. On the other hand, if you want an easiest way to set up an account and transact without getting concerned about its management and operation issues, then opt for a web client. But you must realize that a web client opens up your transactions and funds to counterparty risks because you'll eventually have to share security and control with the owner of the web service. This means that if the wallet of the web service is compromised, as many such cases have been reported, then you risk losing all your funds.

Please note that you can still transact on the bitcoin network as a full client using a smart phone, especially if your phone is based on the Android system. As a mobile client, you may even go ahead and get synchronized with a web or desktop client, and gain a multi-platform wallet that is managed across multiple computing devices, though still retaining a common source of funds.

Having a thorough understanding of the various forms of bitcoin clients will enable you to assess the long-term viability of your preferred option and determine whether you have the capacity to run and manage it. Once you have made a choice, nothing should hinder you from going ahead and investing in bitcoin.

Steps To Investing In Bitcoin

The decentralized nature of bitcoin makes it easier for you to begin trading. The technology continues to evolve to make your trading safer and more enjoyable, so that you can essentially trade from any corner of the world and make more profits. All in all, you can follow the steps below to start trading on the bitcoin network:

Step 1: Creating A Bitcoin Wallet

In this step, you are required to sign up for a bitcoin wallet. A bitcoin wallet is a digital account that will enable you to carry out any transaction on the bitcoin network. With this wallet, you can easily buy, store and sell your bitcoins. Your wallet just acts like a normal universal checking account that you can use to access the bitcoin network. However, starting a bitcoin wallet is easier and takes very few minutes, unlike when you want to start a checking account. You can sign up for your wallet as follows:

- Realize that 3 types of wallets exist: a web wallet and a software wallet. A web wallet is hosted by a third party while a software wallet refers to the type that you will have to install on your own mobile or computing device. With a software wallet, you gain full control of your funds, although you may find it hard to install and maintain such a wallet.

  The market has a variety of wallets to choose from. But remember, your intention is to invest funds into bitcoin. Therefore, make every effort to choose the right bitcoin wallet. If you take this issue lightly, then you risk losing your funds. You can consider the following points before choosing a wallet:

  - ✓ Security of the wallet: This is a critical point that you should not overlook, especially if you're opting for a web wallet. Check the website and ascertain if it has HTTP or HTTPS? In most cases, HTTPS represents a secure protocol. Also, does the wallet offer logins that are secure and strong? Or does it provide a 2FA (two-factor authentication)?

- ✓ Find out if the wallet is reputable or not: Aren't you looking for a wallet that is on the up and up? So, go to the internet forums, such as Bitcoin Forum or bitcoin Reddit, and find out your peers views and perceptions about the wallet. You may go further and ask your peers if they have ever used the wallet and what their experience was.

- ✓ How to back up your wallet: Is the wallet provider offering you any backup options? Does the backup contain data encryption? Is there a backup restoration process? Is this restoration process as easy to use as possible? Ensure you get the right answers to these questions before you start to load your wallet with bitcoin.

- ✓ The wallet's user experience: The wallet should be easy to use. Ensure it is as simple as possible and does not require a lot of experience for you to use it comfortably. Sometimes, your intended use of the bitcoins will determine the type of wallet you would go for. For instance, you may discover that there's a wallet that is best suited for mobile devices, which can work well for a beginner. But as you become an advanced user, downloading a full bitcoin client to your personal computer may be the best alternative. Also, storing your bitcoin offline using wallet hardware devices would be a better idea, if you are eager to engage a more hardened approach.

- ✓ Anonymity: Some wallet providers may ask you to register before transacting, while others may just accept minimal registration information. You may also encounter cases where you are required to undergo user verification processes, like Know Your Customer (KYC) processes, etc. These are some of the issues that you must put in mind, especially if anonymity is an important issue to you.

✓ Transparency: Find out if the wallet provider is as transparent as possible. Can you tell who they are and how they operate? How about the wallet code; is it open source? Remember, peer reviews and vulnerability checks can be easily conducted on an open source code. Also, the source code should be kept up to date. If any of the above issues isn't answered satisfactorily, then you can't be sure that your wallet provider is committed to securing your bitcoins. Besides, you don't want to risk watching helplessly while the exchange runs away with your funds! Therefore, ensure it is as trustworthy as much as possible.

✓ Is address reuse being promoted by the address? Simply put, find out whether the wallet is Hierarchical Deterministic (HD) or not. Remember, HD wallets employ the constant use of new bitcoin addresses; a move that enhances user privacy. As you start using wallets, you'll realize that user privacy remains an important issue that affects many users of the bitcoin network. Therefore, a deterministic wallet has a well-rounded architecture that enhances user protection.

✓ Can you own your bitcoin? Your wallet provider should allow you to gain access to the private keys for your bitcoin wallet. A bitcoin private key refers to a key (just like the physical key) that is normally in form of a 256 bit number and can enable you to gain access to your bitcoin. An example of a private key could be in the form of

16qy2iLQ7d4MiEkKWYau6mfRNHUGZ3NzHz.
The surest way to have control over your bitcoin is to possess your wallet's private key. With the private key, you can as well back up your wallet, in other ways apart from the wallet service.

- ✓ The wallet should have a multi-signature ("Multisig") option: This option is an extra security measure that helps you to secure your bitcoin from attackers and theft. With a "Multisig" feature, a bitcoin transaction will require more than one key to authorize and validate it. This means that more parties must be consulted before the funds can be spent. To explain further, the "Multisig" feature resembles a lock box, which requires the presence of at least 2 parties having different keys that must be used to open the lock box.

- ✓ Liquidity: This is a critical issue, especially if you have a vision of becoming a large bitcoin trader. You will need a wallet or exchange that has a high liquidity and an elaborate market depth in order to perform your activities without any restrictions.

You can go to Bitcoin.com and get their official wallet, or any other wallet that suits your desktop or mobile platforms. Sites like Hivewallet.com, Blockchain.info, Kraken, Coinmkt.com and Coinbase.com are also some of the examples of reputable, reliable and user-friendly sites that you can use a beginner to create your first wallet.

Also, please feel free to use a variety of wallets for different purposes, so that you are not limited in the way you perform your online transactions. This is because many wallets may appear to have similar features even though they can only perform specific functions while possessing peculiar drawbacks. For instance, Hive only operates on Mac platforms though it contains an app store that links up with other bitcoin services. Further, Armory wallet is designed specifically to cater for your enhanced security. However, Hive wallet may work well for you as a beginner and both of these wallets may have unique installation quirks.

Once you've established the authenticity of your prospective wallet provider and are confident that your bitcoins can be safe in their custody, you can create your wallet using the steps below:

- You can create a software wallet as follows:
    - Run a google search for the bitcoin software wallet.
    - Make sure you download the original wallet. In this case, you may go for Bitcoin Core, because it has been thoroughly scrutinized and modified to include more enhanced security features.

        After installing the software, the bitcoin client will be prompted to run a search for the network and initiate the process of downloading the bitcoin blockchain. This may take a few minutes, so be patient and wait for the process to be completed. Remember, you must ensure all the blocks are available in the chain before you can start sending or receiving any transaction.
    - Some wallets take up less hard drive space. These are called lightweight wallets and appear to be easy to use for most beginners. Installing such a wallet may be a good idea because it won't download the full version of the block chain but will work at a faster speed. This is because only a small portion of the blockchain is used at a time, thereby increasing its speed of operation. Electrum is one of these lightweight wallets. However, please note that such wallets are not very secure.
- You may set up a web wallet as well. Remember, a web wallet will store all your private keys on their server, which is often hosted by a third party and controlled by a various people. This makes it a bit popular, because you can access it anywhere. You may also get a wallet that conveniently links both your software and mobile wallets. However, the website can actually 'steal' your bitcoins since they have control over your keys. Again, many web wallets are prone to serious security breaches; therefore, make sure you are aware of such risks before you can begin to invest your funds. Setting up a web-based wallet is such an easy process as follows:

- Search for your wallet of choice after launching the Google Play Store. You could use any search engine that you're comfortable with.

- Install the wallet app and open it after installation.

- Click on "create a new wallet" and proceed to settings and select "backup."

- You'll need a pen and a piece of paper. Select "Master seed backup."

- You'll be asked to undertake a verification process. Please follow the instructions that will be given.

- Then, click on "Set pin code." You'll be required to enter your pin, preferably of six digits.

- You'll be asked to confirm your pin, as well. This essentially means that you have set up your account. So, begin scrolling through the app to familiarize yourself with the various features of your new wallet. You can start sending, receiving, buying or selling bitcoins by just tapping on the balance tab and selecting the action of your choice.

- Remember, if you are interested in having anonymous wallets, you can get them online as well. However, most of these wallets are less secure and can't offer much in terms of insurance. Besides, such servers fluctuate constantly in stability of your coins and are vulnerable to becoming hacked from time to time. Dark wallet is an example of anonymous wallet and it operates as a chrome extension.

  Please keep in mind that a wallet is simply a collection of addresses and the corresponding keys that you can use to unlock the funds within. Therefore, there's absolutely no limit to the number of addresses you can create, as long as such a move helps you keep enhancing your online privacy. And if your wallet allows you to change addresses as often as possible, then you don't have to risk your funds by signing up for an anonymous wallet.

- Once you have set up your wallet, you can start receiving some bitcoins. This can be done in a number of ways. For instance, if you want to receive bitcoin from a sender who is within your vicinity, you can just call out the address (which is the number shown on your screen) or even just scan the QR code. But if the sender is far away, just select the address and copy it to the clipboard before pasting and sending it to the prospective sender. You may also click on "share address via" and select your preferred method, from the options that will show up.

- You can also send bitcoin to other users. You can achieve this by simply scanning the QR code or by just entering the address manually. Please check and choose the correct option between bitcoin (BTC) and USD before entering the amount. You'll see the sign "USD or BTC" on the top right corner of your phone, which you can just tap to make your intended choice. You'll also have to select the transaction fee. This is normally indicated as the "miner fee." Normally, the speed at which the bitcoins get to the recipient determines the amount of the miner fee. If you want it be transferred as fast as possible, you will incur higher charges. This essentially makes the miner fee to be a trade-off between time and cost.

Sometimes you may want to store your bitcoin for a later use. This approach is normally employed when practicing the speculative buying and selling strategy of investing in bitcoin. In such a case, it is not a good idea to store bitcoin in online wallets, mobile apps, computer wallets or exchanges. Therefore, let's look at how you can store bitcoin for long term investment:

Long Term Storage Of Bitcoin

It is important to consider the security of your funds if you want to store your bitcoin for long term use. The security issue is even more critical if you are planning to store large amounts of bitcoin. For instance, you will notice that your bitcoin exchange has an instant withdrawal feature and is also a steward over numerous amounts of bitcoins.

Therefore, you need to come up with a stringent measure that can help in minimizing the possibility of having any intruder stealing your bitcoin in case there is a security breach. As such, it is a good idea to consider adopting cold storage as a necessary security precaution.

Cold storage simply means that you will keep a reserve of bitcoins offline. In that, you have to ensure that your bitcoin is not available on the web or any other computing device. However, it is a good idea to leave a small amount of bitcoin on the server to take care of those expected withdrawals.

You can use the following methods for cold storage of bitcoin:

- Storing on a hardware wallet: This is a tamper-proof electronic device that is meant for the offline storage of the private keys of your coins. The private keys and digital signatures that you will need before spending bitcoins are normally created through this wallet. As you acquire your hardware wallet, please remember to write down the recovery phrase (seed word) on paper then store it safely. Treat this the way you treat your money! Consider making two to three copies and distributing it. By getting your keys offline, you will have completely eliminated the possibility of getting hacked.

  Various hardware wallets have different features that make them unique and safer. For instance, some wallets have a little digital screen that contains a user interface while others have security grid cards that can be used to perform verification processes of your bitcoin transactions.

  The greatest advantage of using a hardware wallet is that even if you accidentally damage or lose it, you just need the recovery phrase and you will easily restore your bitcoins. Further, an intruder cannot transfer bitcoins from your wallet unless they've access to your secret pin. And no Trojan or spy screen recorder can record anything taking place on your wallet, because it has a dedicated LCD screen and doesn't use your computer or system resources.

Due to high demand, most hardware wallets have a waiting period of over a month; so you need to order yours in good time to avoid inconveniences. There are many hardware wallets in the market. Some of the most popular are:

o **Trezor**: This is a secure bitcoin storage and transaction signing tool that pioneered the era of hardware wallets. Trezor uses a deterministic wallet structure and can accommodate unlimited number of keys. It has a distinctive way of entering pin, which helps ensure that keyloggers cannot record it, just in case you use it on a compromised computer. You can set an encryption passphrase on top of the PIN and use more passphrases for plausible deniability.

o **Ledger Nano S**: This product of a France-based startup has a sleek and attractive European look. It has a backup seed key that you can use to recover your bitcoin. Also, it has a an OLED interface that is easy to use and a flash drive like feel that contains two buttons on the side that you can use to navigate the interface. The Ledger Nano S is a battery-less device that can be connected to a mobile device or PC through the USB. It is considered to be the cheapest even though it supports other eight cryptocurrencies at the moment.

o **Keepkey**: This wallet is bigger than Ledger Nano S and Trezor. Therefore, you may find it a bit bulky. Currently, it supports six cryptocurrencies though it works just like the other wallets.

• Storing on a paper wallet: You can also use paper wallets to keep your bitcoin safe. A paper wallet can be described as a document that has both copies of the private and public keys that constitute a wallet. In most cases, a paper wallet will have QR codes, which allow you to make a transaction by just scanning them quickly and adding the keys into your software wallet.

A paper wallet can't be subjected to hardware failures or cybercrimes because there is no digital storage of the keys. However, always exercise more caution while creating your paper wallet because your password can leak other parties. Also, you shouldn't lose your paper wallet, as this essentially means that you also risk losing your money. You can create a paper wallet as follows:

- o In your browser, open BitAddress.org in order to generate a new address.

- o You will be asked to randomly type characters in a form or just move your cursor around in order to create some randomness.

- o Both your private and public keys will be presented to you. At this juncture, you should not scan them.

- o Next, click on the 'Paper wallet' tab and select the number of addresses you want to generate.

- o You may click on "Hide art?" button, especially if you're not interested in keeping the bitcoin artwork.

- o Next, begin creating your new wallets by clicking on the "Generate" button.

- o As soon as you generate your wallet, you can make a hard copy by clicking the "Print" button.

- o You'll be prompted to select the printer you want to use. If you are using a Google Chrome browser, you will also have an opportunity to save the page as a PDF file.

- o Note down the public addresses or you can scan the QR code of the public address in your bitcoin app so that you can begin depositing funds.

If you are using the Blockchain.info website, you can go to the basic paper wallet option and look for the 'Paper wallet' link on the left-hand menu after clicking on the 'Import/Export' option. Bitcoinpaperwallet.com can also give you a more sophisticated paper wallet option. You will get a design of paper wallet that is tamper-resistant and you can order holographic labels that indicate whether the wallet has been tampered with or not. You will be given a live-boot Ubuntu CD that has a pre-installed paper-wallet as well. You can also take the following measures to make your wallet more secure:

o   Ensure no one sees you when creating your wallet.

o   The advantage of using BitAddress is that it supports the encryption of private keys via a unique BIP38 algorithm that provides your wallet with two factor authentication. However, this means that you must use the same website in order to get the private key decrypted.

o   Using a clean operating system will help you avoid the risk of any kind of spyware monitoring your activities. You can create a DVD or USB flash drive that contains a "LiveCD" Linux distribution, like Ubuntu.

o   After using a website to set up a paper wallet, the website code can still run offline. Therefore, you should take your computer offline before you can start creating both the public and private keys.

o   Using a printer that is not connected to the network will also ensure you get ultra-tight security for your paper wallet.

o   Laminate your paper wallet to enhance its durability and proof against water. Storing it in a sealed plastic bag is also a good idea.

o   If possible, you may as well store your paper wallet in a safe to protect it from fire and theft. You can also consider entrusting the paper wallet with a solicitor; this can be the same person that you trust to hold your last will or testament.

o   Storing your wallet in several locations will also enhance redundancy. You can use deposit boxes or even trusted family members.

Once you've created your wallet, remember to keep your password safe. Keep it away from your wallet identifier as much as possible. Furthermore, it is prudent to keep downloading a backup each and every time you receive a transaction or login, and safeguarding it as much as you can. You can also start building your own hardware wallet, especially after becoming more tech-savvy.

Armed with your secure wallet, it's now time to transact on bitcoin. For a new transaction, you may be required to pay a minimum of 0.01 BTC as a transaction fee.

Step 2: Connect Your Wallet To Your Bank Account

This step involves filling your wallet with bitcoins. To accomplish this step, you will have to provide your exchange with the financial details of your real-world bank account in the same way you would do if you were signing up for any online payment service, like when creating a PayPal account.

You will have to provide such details as your full name as it appears on your bank account, the routing number for the account as well as the account number. You can get this information on your paper checks or on your online banking account.

Different exchanges will have different procedures. Just follow the instructions and complete the process as requested. However, the procedure will take the form of:

This example is based on the Coinbase exchange.

- Login and open the Payment Methods page.

- Select "Link a bank account."

- Therefore, go ahead and select your bank from the above options. If your bank is not listed, just click on "Other Bank."

- Once one of the listed banks is selected, a login screen that is specific to your bank will show up.

- Please enter your online username and password as requested, in order to complete the one-time verification process. Different banks have different security procedures. So follow the instructions as directed. Some banks may ask you to answer additional security questions, like entering your PIN. You will notice how simple, secure and fast the verification. All the information you enter in this step, like your username and password, is not stored on Coinbase; rather it is deleted immediately after your bank account's verification process is completed.

  However, should you be uncomfortable sharing your online banking username and password, then proceed by selecting "Other Bank" option from the main menu before choosing the Deposit Verification process. However, you will have to be patient for two to three days to allow this process to be completed.

- Selecting the "Other Bank" option prompts the system to ask for your bank's account name, the bank account number and the bank's routing number. That's not all; you will be asked to enter or select the type of the account that you would like to link, i.e., whether it is business checking, savings or checking.

- After entering your account details, you can carry on with the process using the "instant account verification" (where you will be prompted to enter your online banking credentials) or the "deposit verification" process.

- Two small test deposits will be initiated to your account by the deposit verification procedure. A debit for the combined amount will be initiated as well.

- The deposits should reach your account within two to three days. So proceed to your "Payment Methods" page and verify the account. Just click on the red "verify" button. The verification window will appear; where you can enter the two deposit amounts and complete the process by clicking on "Verify Deposit Amounts."

At this juncture, your bank account is verified and you can start buying bitcoin.

- Feel free to add or charge your credit or debit card (MasterCard or Visa) directly, even when purchasing bitcoin. The funds that you purchase through such an option are normally credited to your account immediately.

Also, some exchanges may allow you to withdraw USD from your wallet through a bank wire or into your linked account. Others may also allow you to place a sell order, in which case your USD proceeds are paid to your PayPal or linked account.

Remember, linking your bank account to your bitcoin wallet could pose a great risk to your personal security as well as your online shopping. So, as a prerequisite, ensure your exchange or wallet provider guarantees high standards for security and encryption. Else, you could become an easy target for many online hackers and scammers.

Step 3: Using Funds In Your Bank Account To Buy Bitcoin

This is a pretty easy step that involves purchasing bitcoin and adding it to your wallet. Once you get to your wallet page, you will see an option that is labelled "Buy Bitcoin" or something close to that. Therefore, just click this option and follow the directions that will be given in order to purchase your first bitcoin, using the money in your bank account.

However, you can still buy bitcoins if you don't want to use your wallet or if you want to be as anonymous as possible. This means that you can buy bitcoin from anywhere around the world, through such options as brokers, local traders, ATM and even Gift cards. Under such circumstances, your ability to buy bitcoin will be based on:

- Your place of residence: Even though buying bitcoin from across the globe is possible, always look for the options that are readily available in your country. For instance, USA and Canada remain to be the biggest markets for bitcoin, and as a buyer, you will find a wide variety of options of bitcoin trading. Exchanges (like Bitstamp; Coinbase's GDAX and Bitfinex), peer-to-peer markets (like Bitsquare Bitquick, Paxful and LocalBitcoins) and direct exchanges (Kraken and Coinbase) are some of the most common options. Please note that purchases made on exchanges are cheaper than those on peer-to-peer markets.

- The method of payment: In most cases, buying bitcoin involves sending money to another person. This means that if your country has a better and more advanced financial system, then you can easily exchange your money for bitcoin. Always keep in mind that the fiat currency has proved to be the main hindrance in the flow of bitcoin trading. Therefore, using a slow and expensive payment channel means that acquiring bitcoin will also be slow and expensive. But using a payment channel that's fast makes your purchase of bitcoin easier and less expensive. Your exchange will always direct you on the preferred methods of payment. For instance, most exchanges accept bank transfers but would not let you use the common private payment channels, such as cash, Western-Union, etc., to buy bitcoin. Also, a few vendors may accept PayPal or credit cards. This is because, while bitcoin transactions are irreversible, PayPal or credit card transactions can be reversed.

- The amount of private information that you would like to disclose: In most jurisdictions, bitcoin is always subject to financial regulation. As such, anti-money laundering (AML) rules are constantly being applied to platforms that sell bitcoins or those that enable users to transact with bitcoin. A majority of these platforms are forced to come up with mechanisms to verify the identity of their customers, such as adopting the Know Your Customer (KYC) rules. The fact that bitcoin transactions are normally saved publicly on the blockchain and can be traced back implies that the level of private information you reveal while buying bitcoins can have serious ramifications on your personal privacy. Consequently, several exchanges have different grades of KYC based on the amount of private information that you must disclose. Notable grades are:

✓ No KYC grade: This is the lowest. In this grade, the platform doesn't need to know who you are. You won't have to produce any form of identification and you can purchase bitcoins through any private means, such as by using Western-Union, Paysafecard, MoneyGram or cash. Some jurisdictions may allow you to buy bitcoins without KYC, e.g., Gift cards, bitcoin ATMs and on the peer-to-peer marketplaces like Localbitcoins. But it is important to note that buying bitcoin without KYC is more expensive than using other options.

✓ KYC light grade: This level of KYC uses your phone numbers or your payment channel to carry out your online identity. Thus, by making payments using the common means of payment such as your credit card, PayPal or bank account, it simply means that your identity is already known by your payment provider. However, most platforms, whether marketplaces, exchange platforms or direct exchanges, will only allow you to buy limited amount of bitcoin using the KYC light grade.

✓ The full KYC grade: With this grade, you'll be required to identify yourself as fully as possible. In that, you'll be asked to provide extra documents on top of verifying your identity using your phone numbers and your bank account, in order to provide a more precise and perfect proof of your identity. The additional documents may involve one or a combination of such documents as a utility bill, a driver's license, an ID card or a passport, and some platforms may even ask you to provide formal approvals of your documents of identification from a trusted third party, like a bank, or a notary. Your exchange can even demand that you take part in the process of video identification or just submit a photo that shows you holding your ID card. Remember, full KYC becomes mandatory when trading on exchanges or when investing large sums of money.

The above factors will help you determine the platform that best suits your needs and you'll notice that the process of buying bitcoin is a lot easier than you ever imagined. But be cautious; as a beginner, don't jeopardize your investments by taking unnecessary risks! Instead, start small and grow slowly as you master the art of trading with bitcoin.

Once you've acquired your first bitcoin, you can begin to trade as well. This is the step that requires most of your ingenuity and utilizes your steadfastness in order to make some profits and change the trajectory of your financial status.

Step 4: Trading With Bitcoin

After acquiring your first bitcoin, you can begin by using it to buy goods and services. This is a very critical step that can help you understand how trading with bitcoin works. So, go ahead and find out if your favorite websites accept bitcoin. At the moment, an increasing number of retailers are beginning to accept bitcoin as a method of payment.

For exa9mple, you can use bitcoin to make computer purchases at Newegg.com. Or just visit CheapAir.com and book your plane ticket from the comfort of your bed! Other online vendors that accept bitcoin are: Whole Foods, Zappos, Subway, Victoria's Secret, Bitcoin.travel, Overstock.com, Wordpress, Amazon, etc. You can go to bitcoin.org and do a further research about specific services that are listed as well as acquainting yourself with various terms and conditions. Also, try to access coinmap.org's handy map of physical locations and identify those vendors that are within your locality and accept bitcoin.

As you become more tech-savvy, start buying bitcoin when its price is low before purchasing your favorite goods when the value of bitcoin is high. This way, you can generate value for yourself by simply keeping the goods or selling them to make a profit.

Since the bitcoin market is still new, highly fragmented and exhibiting huge spreads, indulging in bitcoin trading can be an extremely profitable venture. Bitcoin's volatility alongside its protracted history of bubbles has played a significant role in attracting new users and investors to the cryptocurrency. With each new bubble, an earth-shattering hype is created that puts bitcoin's name in the news. Consequently, this media attention makes masses to get interested in bitcoin, up to when the hype dies away.

Thus, every time the price of bitcoin rises, speculators as well as new investors stand a chance to reap big in profits. Remember, bitcoin is a global currency that is easy to send, irrespective of where you are. This means that trading bitcoin is such a simple exercise that you can't wait for any prompting before diving in. So, since you have some bitcoins in your wallet, you can start trading as soon as possible; because undergoing verification processes may no longer be necessary.

The following are some of the ways to carry out bitcoin trading:

1: Bitcoin CFDs (Contracts for Difference)

This form of bitcoin trading allows you to trade bitcoin without using bitcoin itself. CFDs can help you gain exposure to bitcoin even though you are yet to own it physically. With a CFD, you can take risks with the fluctuating prices of fast-moving international financial markets or instruments, like commodities, currencies, treasuries, indices, and shares.

Basically, a bitcoin Contracts For Difference represents a contract between the exchange and you, the trader, whereby both of you agree to pay each other any difference as prices rise or fall in cash, instead of having the physical goods (bitcoin) delivered. In this case, your CFD will declare that any difference between your entry and exit price automatically constitutes your profit or loss. In a nutshell, a CFD refers to an agreement, which is normally held between two parties simulating as if the actual physical asset, in this case bitcoin, is in the trader's custody.

For instance, you may sign a CFD with a reputable exchange such as Plus500 for bitcoin at today's prices, and set the contract to end at 10pm (most likely due to the fact that bitcoin trading at Plus500 has to come to an end by 10pm). Resultantly, the value to be traded will be determined by the current price of bitcoin, and in the meantime, you can set a contract time, say a number of hours into the future, which represents the point at which either the buyer (you) or the seller (the exchange) gets to be paid any difference.

This essentially means that if your intuition about the fluctuating bitcoin prices turns out to be correct, with the price changes occurring within the set time frame, then the trading company will pay you the difference. But if your intuition turns out to be incorrect and bitcoin prices fail to drop or rise as you had expected, then you will have to suffer a loss by paying the difference to the exchange or the trading company. With this form of trading, ideally, you and the exchange are basically betting on whether or not there will be a rise or a drop in bitcoin prices.

However, bitcoin CFD trading can be such a risky undertaking. So, get some experience first; try to understand bitcoin's market volatility before making such a move.

Remember, undertaking bitcoin CFD trading is also laced with various outcomes: both positive and negative. Let's explore some of them.

Advantages of CFD trading

Below are some of the benefits of CFD trading:

- CFD trading is more flexible because you can either go long (where you bet that there will be an increase in price) or short (where you bet that there will be a drop in price). Further, bitcoin CFD trading can be undertaken on any day and at any time. You can also close CFD trades whenever it is deemed possible.

- No need to hold the actual bitcoin. Therefore, you won't have to waste any time trying to secure the bitcoins that you would have bought. Eventually, the risk of losing your bitcoin is completely eliminated.

- Leveraging: Would you like to control a larger position even though you have a smaller capital? Then CFD trading will help you realize your goal. As a skilled trader, this technique may still see you make more profits even during those times the markets aren't moving as much. However, with leveraging, your risk is multiplied; so you need to be cautious about it as well.

- Shorting the market: Indeed, you may encounter some exchanges that can allow you to short the market. However, you will notice that setting up a short position while carrying out bitcoin CFD trading is the easiest of them all. This means that if you're convinced that the price of bitcoin will certainly drop, then you can just short the cryptocurrency by opening a sell/short trade; something that you can't do when holding the physical bitcoin. Thus, you essentially gain more flexibility, especially in terms of your trading strategy.

- Lower taxes: In most jurisdictions, profits earned from bitcoin CFD trading attract lower tax rates than those earned from buying and selling bitcoin directly. This is because, platforms that facilitate CFD trading are more regulated and secure than most exchanges.

- Execution speed: Bitcoin CFDs have the fastest execution speed. Remember, exchanges depend on volume. Therefore, if many people are not trading, your order cannot get filled. But with CFDs, brokers are normally plugged into liquidity providers, thereby offering guaranteed and often prompt execution. Simply put, with CDF trading, individuals don't have to trade with each other over a particular exchange, but you're guaranteed full access to liquidity from institutional partners, thereby making transactions faster. As a result, you can quickly respond to any dynamic trend in the market.

- High trading frequency and strategies that are quite automated: You may also come across some bitcoin brokers, like Whaleclub, that can provide you with a full API. This implies that then you can build some custom scripts to trade, especially if you possess some developing experience. Furthermore, another broker that is known as Evolve Markets, can enable you undertake scalping and high frequency trading via their MT4 client. Please note that this form of trading is rarely common on most bitcoin exchanges because they are not designed to handle such a heavy load.

Disadvantages of CFD trading

Implementing CFD trading may affect you in the following ways:

- Initially, CFDs may appear to be attracting low fees when compared to other methods of trading. However, these fees are always higher than those charged by those exchanges that facilitate the direct buying and selling of bitcoin, like Kraken or Bitstamp.

  For instance, on top of the daily interest on open positions, fees at Plus500 are derived from the spread, which is essentially the difference between the price at which you buy (i.e. the asking price) and the price at which you sell (i.e. the bidding price). You may end up incurring loses that range from as low as 0.5% to as high as 5% of the traded sum. Still, you might be charged a commission over and above the spread, which grossly affects your overall earnings.

- Also, as a long term trader, bitcoin CFDs may not work well for you. You will have to incur a certain cost, which is commonly known as a Premium, in order to maintain an open trade while using CFDs. The Premium normally takes 0.1% of your position daily. Remember, leveraging on a CFD is facilitated by loans made from the exchange to trader. Therefore, the whole duration of this financing agreement attracts some interest charges. On the other hand, had you chosen to go for the physical bitcoins, you would just hold them in a digital wallet for a given duration without incurring any costs.

- With CFDs, you can't escape the dreaded "margin call." The financing arrangement associated with CFDs makes exchanges look for stringent measures to protect themselves against unforeseen, drastic moves within the market. Unfortunately, these measures will always place your balances into the negative deep figures. This means, whenever there is a high leverage; markets experience high volatility as well as a frenetic trading pace that makes such negative balances a substantial risk. In reality, arising losses are always the liability of the trader, but if you are unable to bear them, then your exchange will have to suffer those financial losses. Therefore, as a precautionary measure, your exchange is likely to close you out before your balance becomes negative, a phenomenon commonly referred to as a margin call. A margin call can be defined as the act of your exchange closing your trade due to the fact that your money or investment isn't that sufficient to cover your loss. But if your margin account is better-funded, you are less likely to attract a margin call. So, in the midst of any market volatility, if your margin buffer is too thin, you may end up being knocked out of the trade at a loss. Sometimes margin calls can be annoying, especially if they occur on your trade that had a potential of becoming more profitable.

Bitcoin CFDs can be quite challenging, since you may realize that the profits you hoped for aren't just coming. This means that you must keep yourself constantly informed in order to keep understanding the significance of major market events. But as a beginner, this could be just the right opportunity to discover how bitcoin CFDs work and whether CFD trading can be a profitable venture or not.

Getting Started With CFDS

If you feel you have the stamina to try out bitcoin CFD trading, then the following steps will help you achieve your objective:

- Begin by experimenting with CFDs: Many Bitcoin CFD brokers, such as Fortrade, AvaTrade and Plus500, provide a demo trading program that resembles their regular trading interface. The actual price of bitcoin as well as the overall operations of the CFDs is real, although your trading account gets to be automatically filled with simulated money. Use the demo as long as you can, provided that you gain enough confidence. Plus500 is one of the simplest trading platforms that can help you learn how to do CFD trading. So begin by signing up for your demo account as soon as possible. Got to Plus500's website, click the "Start Trading Now!" button and download and install the Plus500 demo.

  Click on the "Download Now!" button and go on to follow the steps as indicated.

  Once the application is fully installed, please run it and register as a new user after selecting the "Demo Mode." You have to enter an email address and a password. Note this information since you'll need it for signing-in in the future.

  As a new user, you must remain in the "Demo Mode" until you can fully understand the important features of CFDs. This will also help you to assess your intended profitability through real-time demonstration. The guiding principle should be the fact that if you can't achieve fairly consistent profits in simulated trading, there is no guarantee that you'll be successful while using real money.

- Next, log in to start trading: Once the sign-in panel shows up, you can demo-trade by just clicking on the link "Try our web trader in your browser." But if you feel more confident and would like to use the application that you've downloaded, just enter your email address and password and click "submit."

- Now you need to locate and examine bitcoin CFDs: Just go to the leftmost pane and enter "bitcoin" in the search field. Bitcoin will appear in the instrument pane. Clicking on the Details link will lead to the display of important information on bitcoin CFDs. By moving the cursor over the "?" icons, you can see various tooltips accompanied by their associated information.

  The Details panel may indicate that there's an applicable charge of 0.1% of each contract owned. This charge is normally due at midnight. Also, your funds are leveraged 13 times. Meaning, whenever there's a $1 movement in the underlying price of bitcoin, there's a subsequent $13 movement in the value of each contract you hold.

  The initial margin normally refers to the percentage of the total value of your position that your account must be having before opening the trade. For instance, in this case, you're required to have a deposit of 8% of the value. The maintenance margin simply entails the prerequisite percentage so that your trade can remain open. Remember, should your position drop in value, your initial margin may drastically drop below your maintenance margin and lead to the closing of the trade (a margin call). Also, take note of the expiry date of the contract, i.e. mid-June 2018 in our case. This means that any position maintained until then will just be closed out.

- You can start trading: Having understood the contract, buying and selling bitcoin isn't a struggle. Just go to the Detail or Instrument pane and click on "short" or "buy", if you're expecting the price to rise or fall respectively.

  So, go ahead and structure and enter your trade. However, avoid selling more bitcoin contracts than you own; else, you'll be creating a short position.

  Buying the equivalent number of contracts will help you close a short positon.

  The system will determine the current value of the total number of the selected contracts and convert that value into your local currency. The necessary initial margin will be determined and converted as well.

The options, "close at loss" and "close at profit", may be ticked and fixed to form a stop loss and a profit target, in that order. So, when prices of bitcoin reach these levels, the app automatically closes your position. This implies that you can automate the process of taking profits on good trades while limiting losses on your bad trades. The stop option is meant to ensure that the trade is closed whenever the price falls below your stop-loss level.

In addition, you can apply the "trailing stop" option when the price is trending. With the trailing stop option, you set the stop-loss price at a certain dollar amount that's less than the prevailing market price instead of setting it at a single, absolute dollar amount.

If the price moves against your expected direction, the trade automatically gets closed depending on the selected number of "Pips." Pips refer to decimal places in Forex trade. You don't have to worry about this; just use the arrows or number field to get the value entered before the trailing stop extent shows up as a percentage.

Lastly, you can use the *"Only buy / sell when rate is* [x]" option to get a long or short trade automatically entered once the price of bitcoin reaches a given level.

- Start checking your balance, closed positions, orders as well as open positions: 3 tabs along the top of your trading interface are very instrumental in your attempts to access the history and the status of your trading positions. Also, the "Funds Management" menu on the toolbar can help you access your account balance and other related details.

- Continue exploring and examining other major features: For example, just close to the Details link there's a bell icon. You can click on it to activate the Price Alert feature and start receiving email or SMS alerts when a certain price of bitcoin is reached.

- Finally fund your account and start trading: By now you must have built your confidence in CFD trading. So, go ahead and start trading with real money, though I believe you must have already dived deep into it! You can fund your Plus500 account through the following options: Skrill, PayPal, Diner's Club International,

Maestro, MasterCard or Visa.

Never forget that Plus500 bitcoin CFDs trading is still a high-risk, challenging proposition. So you need to put in some extra effort in order to bring in high returns. Always remember that as you embark on CFD trading, you suffer an immediate loss, as a result of the difference between the market price of bitcoin and the price offered by the exchange, when the position is being opened.

Therefore, for you to break even, your only hope is that the price of bitcoin has to move quite an appreciable distance within the direction of your choice, so that this spread can be adequately covered for. For instance, suppose you opened a position by buying bitcoin and immediately closed the same position, you will essentially lose the difference between the buying and the selling price.

Further, bitcoin markets are quite unpredictable and very competitive. Most traders are highly advantaged in resources and are more skillful and experienced. So, as a beginner, your experience will be more adventurous than that of wading into deep, shark-filled waters. For this reason, stick with the Demo Mode up to when you are strong enough to survive.

Slowly build the discipline, patience and skill. Keep on studying and practicing. Never forget to keep a trading journal as well. You need to take note of the pertinent facets of your trading experience and record them. Record your mood and try to find out whether your risk tolerance is improving or not.

Bitcoin Day Trading

You employ this technique when you focus on trading only when it is convenient to you and not holding any position while you sleep. Day trading refers to an active involved style of trading that seeks to take advantage of short but significant movements in prices. You can be drawn to bitcoin day trading due to the fact:

- The volatility of bitcoin remains much higher than other trading instruments. Therefore, the bitcoin market is full of plenty of tradeable action that you can capitalize on. Until now, bitcoin has rarely had dull, sideways price action!

- You can benefit from bitcoin even though you don't hold a long-term position nor understand its technical complexities. Essentially, you just trade bitcoin the same way you would do with basic goods.

- You can access leveraged trading on most exchanges. So, if you are eager to gain a lot of exposure to upside and downside risk, especially more than what your ordinary trading budget would allow, the bitcoin day trading will be the best option for you.

- Sometimes, day trading exchanges charge lower fees unlike most traditional exchanges. This means you need to choose your exchange wisely in order to make more profits.

However, you must have some experience before undertaking bitcoin day trading. You will discover that adopting a much long-term trading strategy is easier and more profitable, especially if you can just buy bitcoin at a major low and dispose it a major high, than the day trading strategy. Day trading is more demanding, especially in terms of your time, attention and energy. So it may not work well for you if you already lead a busy lifestyle.

Before getting started with day trading, you must have the following:

- Trading capital: The rule of the thumb is to always day trade with the funds that you're ready to lose because, as a new trader, there are high chances that you can lose your initial trading funds. Starting out with a small amount and allowing yourself some ample time to learn the technique is a better idea.

- A game plan: You need some technical analysis, in order to systematically assess price charts and make quick market decisions. You gain such skills by spending some more time practicing and watching the screen. Remember, practice makes perfect. Also, please learn how to manage your funds properly. By so doing, you can minimize losses that could emanate from wrong calls or maximize your profits when your judgment turns out to be right.

- Bitcoin exchange: Sign up for a good exchange. Go to BuyBitcoinWorldWide and search for an exchange that guarantees low fees, deep liquidity and a more user-friendly interface. Kraken, GDAX, Cex.io and Bitstamp are some of the exchanges that you can find to be more resourceful.

Once you fulfill the above requirements, look for an appropriate time and start trading as soon as possible.

Bitcoin Arbitrage Trading

This form of trading involves less risk than day trading or speculative bitcoin trading. Bitcoin arbitrage trading refers to the simultaneous buying and selling of bitcoin to make profits as a result of price differences on various exchanges. In other words, your main goal is to exploit the differences in price on various exchanges while keeping the change you obtain as free money.

For instance, suppose the bitcoin price on exchange X is USD 9000 while exchange Y offers the same bitcoin at USD 9150, you may choose to capitalize on this and exploit the difference in prices and take the USD 150 for yourself. Thus, you will end up concurrently buying bitcoin on the cheaper exchange and selling it on the expensive one.

Therefore, you must have accounts at more than one bitcoin exchange in order to do arbitrage trading. This will enable you to take advantage of the low and high prices and keep free money as much as possible. Also, don't forget to have some funds in both your fiat currency (USDs) and bitcoin. Try to deposit your bitcoin in the exchange that has the most expensive price of bitcoin and USDs in the exchange that has the cheapest price of bitcoin. Then, try to simplify things by just buying and selling the same amount at the same time.

This form of trading has a few challenges. To begin with, always ensure that the trading fees don't affect your income. For you to make any profit, the difference in the price of bitcoin on the two exchanges should be more than the sum of trading fees on both exchanges. So, keep comparing bitcoin prices on various exchanges and determine the right time to make a smart move.

Another challenge with this form of trading is that other traders and bots might change their price and go in front of you after seeing your bid. You can counter this problem by ensuring that you go ahead of them by just revising your price so that your new price is a dollar less than their price. Don't worry; as long as you get your bitcoin sold, even if in piecemeal, you will still make a profit. This process can be extremely fast, but sometimes it may take long. So, be patient and wait for any opening, since you never know who may be buying or selling simultaneously.

Consider taking a smaller profit faster, especially if liquidity is there and the price difference is large enough, instead of just waiting to trade slowly and get a bigger profit. This enables you to remain active and you may cumulatively make more profits, at the end of the day.

Bitcoin Margin Trading

Margin trading is an extremely profitable but risky trading endeavor. With this form of trading, you can borrow capital (which is usually advanced at high interest rates) in order to boost your leverage. Such borrowing is normally pegged on the hope that things will always go well to guarantee huge gains in terms of profits. Though, sometimes, you can make a wrong move and end up battling the high interest rates, margin calls and even closing the position at a total loss altogether.

The idea behind margin trading is a simple one. You may approach an exchange that offers a leverage of 1:1 and borrow close to 100% of your holdings. For example, if you have a balance of 1 bitcoin, you can be allowed to trade 2 bitcoins, thereby increasing your profit potential. You may even come across other exchanges offering 100:1, 20:1, 3.3:1 or 2.5:1 margins. The 100:1 margin trading can see you either growing 500% in a short time or being liquidated within a twinkle of an eye!

If you are interested in margin trading, you can do it in two ways: Either enter a long position, where you can buy and bet that the bitcoin price will go up, or enter a short position, where you bet that the price will go down. So if you are sure that the price of bitcoin is bound to move in a particular direction, then margin trading can help you capitalize to the fullest on those correct predictions.

All you need is to develop some level of understanding in risk management so that you can get the most out of your leveraged funds. Just start trading with small amounts of money at margins that don't exceed 2:1. Don't use all of your funds in a single transaction. For example, you can put $1,000 of your personal capital into an account, but just use only $100 of this personal capital to margin trade at a 2:1. This means that even if your margin trade doesn't end up being as successful as you had envisaged, you'll still be left with $900 which you can use in other forms of bitcoin trading.

Still, your exchange may cap your margin account with a "maintenance requirement" in order to slow you down from undertaking excessive borrowing. The maintenance requirement just stipulates the least amount that you must have in equity on your account before you can be allowed to undertake further borrowing. All in all, bitcoin margin trading can be a great way to make more money, as long as you have a thorough or even basic understanding of risk management.

Bitcoin Binary Trading

This option provides you with the most dynamic way of improving your financial portfolio. You can either invest in bitcoin via binary options or opt to trade binary options using bitcoin. However, using bitcoin to trade binary options is the better option. This simply means that you will be investing in contracts using your bitcoins.

You will have to predict if the price of a given asset will be lower or higher than the strike price by the end of a given timeframe. Meaning, should your prediction turn out to be correct, then your investments will accrue some profits.

On the other hand, if you choose to invest bitcoin through binary options, it means that you are using your fiat currency to trade bitcoin as a tradable asset. In this case, your aim is to make profits as a result of the foreseen or unforeseen movements in the price of bitcoin.

Generally, you may find binary trading to be fun and enjoyable, especially if you are whacky about betting. Therefore, get a quality, reliable exchange or broker that guarantees a higher percentage payout. Your exchange will present you with a number of binary trading options as well as different types of assets. You can begin by trading on several of these assets and a few types of options, so that you can learn how binary trading works. After some time, go through your records and find out the type of trades that generate more profits. This way, you can begin to specialize in a few of them until you end up with 1 or 2 asset types on 1 or 2 binary options.

Tips For Successful Binary Trading

Remember, some binary option strategies work well with certain assets and option types, particularly due to their unique characteristics. You will learn this more while practicing binary trading. For now, try paying a close attention to the following points:

- Develop strategies and do extensive research: Come up with a system that will help you select when to call or determine how much to invest in each trade. Develop faith in your system; keep investing in it even when you feel nervous about losing. Make a habit of studying the news and relevant market figures before trading. As you become comfortable trading within your system, you will eventually know the type of information you need and where it can be found.

- You may set some rules and stick to them as you trade: Having personal rules will help you avoid making common mistakes and trade consistently in a controlled manner. Your rules may take the form of:
  - Avoid taking an option just because you want it to occur.
  - Trades should be placed at least 15 seconds before the deadlines.
  - Research before trading.
  - Trading should occur when you are undistracted and able to focus.

- Look for a bankroll management strategy: You don't want to lose the total amount of money that's available for trading. Therefore, the amount you invest per trade should ensure that you can survive a bad run.

You can adopt a martingale-staking strategy to enable you to increase your investments when you are on a losing phase so that any win makes you recover your losses. But ensure you have a "stop loss" to avoid losing the whole bankroll.

Likewise, a positive progression staking strategy, which is the opposite of martingale, and increases your stake during a winning phase, will help you risk only a certain fraction of the streak's profits.

Another common technique of managing your bankroll is always withdrawing 50% of your winnings. The other half can be left in the trading account to grow the bankroll. For instance, work out your winnings after 30 days and withdraw 50% of them. You can adjust this figure up or down, depending on other bitcoin demands.

By and large, your binary trading option strategy should be a function of two components: a method of selecting the preferred option and a method of determining how much to invest per trade. Be patient, start small and sample out a few different options. Keep modifying and improving your system as you grow in experience and data. Remember, bitcoin binary trading resembles gambling; it has a higher risk than other forms of bitcoin trading.

Bitcoin trading can be undertaken in so many ways that we cannot exhaust them. Many trading options are being developed by various exchanges in an attempt to make the experience safer and user-friendly. So, keep interacting with your exchange. Find out new opportunities. And together with your exchange, try to customize what's already on offer and come up with a plan that is most befitting to your needs.

However, if bitcoin trading isn't working well for you and you would want to take a break from it, then bitcoin mining can offer the much needed relief. Mining is another lucrative investment that can help you take control of your future. Therefore, in the next chapter, you will learn about the essentials of bitcoin mining and discover how to maximize your earning opportunities albeit skipping the hassle of trading bitcoins.

Bitcoin Mining

Bitcoin mining refers to the process through which transactions get verified and added to the blockchain, as well as the means through which brand new bitcoins are created. Bitcoin mining is normally likened to the usual mining of any precious metal, like gold.

Just like gold, there's simply a limited amount of bitcoin, since there will only ever be a total of 21 million bitcoins, and the more you extract, the more difficult it becomes to find it. The only difference with bitcoin mining is that bitcoins are not necessarily created through mining. Instead, miners are rewarded with bitcoins for validating previous transactions.

The mining process entails compiling recent transactions into different blocks and then attempting to find solutions to a computationally difficult mathematical problem. As a miner, if you're the first one to solve the puzzle, you'll place the next block on the blockchain before claiming the bitcoin rewards.

Initially, bitcoin miners were mainly comprised of cryptography enthusiasts, who were interested in the project and would use their extra computer power to validate the blockchain in order to be rewarded with bitcoins. But due to the ever rising value of bitcoin, many people have been attracted to bitcoin mining and continue to invest in powerful hardware in order to mine as many bitcoins as possible. As a result, bitcoin mining has grown to be very competitive, because with more and more miners coming on board, mining difficulty continues to increase. However, this shouldn't scare you, there's still a chance that you can make money through bitcoin mining.

How To Mine Bitcoins

Keep in mind that bitcoin mining isn't a good investment for everyone. This is because it is becoming increasingly expensive until making a profit is almost impossible. However, if you're a risk taker, the following steps can get you started:

- Determine if bitcoin mining is a profitable venture. Go to Bitcoin mining calculator (99bitcoins.com) and key in the data of the bitcoin miner you intend to buy. This will enable you to run some calculations and approximate how long it will take you to break even and even make a profit. But be prepared to spend a few hundred dollars in order to mine some bitcoins.

  Further, please determine if bitcoin mining is legal in your country. Many countries may not have a problem, especially if you faithfully pay taxes on your earnings. Besides, in the US, many bitcoin mining firms are located in Chelan County, Washington in order to benefit from cheap electricity. Remember, bitcoin mining consumes a lot of power, as well.

- Purchase the bitcoin mining hardware. Get an ASIC miner. ASIC miner is a specialized computer that's designed for the sole purpose of bitcoin mining. Your home desktop or laptop computer can't handle the current bitcoin mining processes.

  You can go through various mining hardware reviews and get a machine that is best for you. If you have enough capital, you can go for, Antminer S9, which is one of the most powerful miners.

  - Join a mining pool and share your harsh rate with other miners. A mining pool involves a group of bitcoin miners that combine computing power to create as many bitcoins as possible. Don't go for solo mining because bitcoins are normally awarded in blocks. The current bitcoin block reward is 12.5. You have to be extremely lucky in order to get any of these coins. Otherwise, if you join a mining pool, it is easier to get this block reward, and if your contribution to the pools hashrate is 1%, then you'll be happy to pocket 0.125 bitcoins.

By joining a pool, you'll be given smaller and easier algorithms to solve. Eventually, your pool's combined effort will ensure that you solve the entire bigger algorithm then earn bitcoins, which are spread out across the pool depending on your individual contribution. In simple terms, the mining pool helps you to make a more consistent amount of bitcoin thereby receiving a good return on your investment. Consider the following points before joining a mining pool:

- o The pool should be stable.

- o Find out how easy it is to withdraw your funds.

- o The fees charged for mining and withdrawal of funds.

- o Find out the reward method.

You may compare your findings with views from bitcoin wiki. Once you make a decision to join a particular pool, sign up and get a username and password.

- Install a mining program. This is a mining client that you run on your computer so that you can control and monitor your mining rig. Most mining programs are open source and readily available for free. Your mining pool may have their own recommended software, so find out what they use and why. Else, there are very many mining programs; just pick one, which is compatible with your rig and install. Check here if you are interested in comparing different mining software.

- Start mining. Just connect your miner to a power outlet and fire it up. In addition, connect your miner to your computer, normally through USB, and open up your mining program. You will be prompted to enter your mining pool, username and password.

After getting this information configured, you can start mining. Just run the batch file that may have been created and let the miner connect and begin to mine. When the miner starts working, you will discover that the rest of your computer will slow to a crawl.

Keep monitoring the temperature, as the mining program may push the hardware to their limits and cause a lot of overheating. Consider making use of such a program as SpeedFan to ensure that your temperatures don't exceed your safe limits.

- Keep checking your profitability: After mining for a while, it's a good idea to check your figures and ascertain whether mining is a good investment or not. A simple way to assess this is to find out how much you made over the last few days. And how does that compare to what you spent in your attempt to keep your equipment running optimally during that time?

Sometimes, you may want to invest in bitcoin mining without going through the trouble of owning and maintaining the mining hardware. In such a case, cloud mining may be your preferred way of investing your funds.

Bitcoin Cloud Mining

Bitcoin cloud mining involves using shared processing power that is run from remote data centers. With cloud mining, you can mine bitcoins without managing the mining hardware; an option that you will find more useful if you are not that technically minded. Cloud mining is offered as a service and the returns are normally low. However, always be careful; cloud mining attracts very many scams.

The following are some of the benefits of cloud mining:

✓ Cloud mining reduces the chances of making losses as a result of the breakdown of mining equipment. You don't have to worry about being let down by equipment suppliers as well.

✓ You won't encounter ventilation problems that arise from hot equipment.

✓ When mining ceases to be profitable, you won't have equipment that you have to sell in order to recover your capital.

✓ You will have a quiet, cooler home, because you won't have fans that are constantly humming and you won't incur extra electricity costs.

On the other hand, cloud mining may not be a worthwhile endeavor because:

✓ There is no flexibility and you won't have control over the process.

✓ You are likely to be bombarded with frequent contractual warnings that mining operations may be terminated due to the price of bitcoin.

✓ Low profit margins. This is because operation costs have to be recovered as of first priority.

✓ You risk being a victim of fraud because mining operations are normally opaque.

✓ And if you are a geek who is mad about system building, cloud mining will be too boring for you!

How Cloud Mining Works

In this case, there is a company, which owns and runs various bitcoin mining hardware located in different areas where the cost of power is low. This company then offers some of its processing power for rent to different people for a fee. Your earnings are dependent on the amount of hash power that you rent.

The following are some of the companies that offer bitcoin cloud mining:

- **Minergate**: With Minergate, you can withdraw as little as 0.01 bitcoins while mining coins with the highest exchange rate.

- **Genesis mining**: This is the largest and most transparent cloud mining provider. Genesis keeps investing in the best available hardware in order to continue offering better services to investors.

- **Eobot**: If you are looking for the easiest and cheapest cloud mining solutions, Eobot can help you get started. You will be allowed to exchange between any cryptocurrency as well as undertaking free mining and you can.

- **HASHING 24 (Bitfury)**: Their aim is to get everyone involved in bitcoin mining. You can access the latest technology while undertaking large scale mining of bitcoin.

Once you have put the above issues into consideration and still feel confident that you can make some money by investing in cloud mining, just start by simply buying shares online and joining a cloud mining pool. Just select your preferred plan, make the necessary payments and start mining.

Always perform background checks before investing. You may try to talk to former customers or carry out your investigations on social media channels in order to establish the authenticity of the operators you come across. It is all about performing due diligence just the same way you do for any other investment.

But don't forget that the risk of fraud and mismanagement is too common in this kind of arrangement. Therefore, only invest in cloud mining if you are comfortable with such risks, and don't invest more than you are willing to lose!

You can earn some bitcoins from mining; but remember it's more profitable to buy than to mine bitcoins. If you believe mining is cool and you would want to experiment with it, then cloud mining isn't the best option. Instead, buying a cheap USB miner and running it at home will prove more profitable in the long run.

Tips For Investing In Bitcoin

Bitcoin's high volatility in price range coupled with its ease of buying makes it the most sought after investment option across the globe. Many customers continue to be drawn to it, with the aim of benefiting in one way or another. However, this doesn't happen without a considerable share of risks. Therefore, the following tips are meant to help you trade safely and avoid making common mistakes:

- Understand the market before trading. This is a continuous process that requires a lot of time, focus and effort. It is important to undertake a thorough market research and be up to date with current market trends. Part of your research may involve consulting financial or investment experts and establishing a workable plan Ask as many questions as you can and only make a move when you are confident it is the right one.

  Sometimes, your exchange may be running promotions and issuing coupons; always take advantage of such incentives.

- Sometimes, the price of bitcoin may vary from one country or region to another. If you have a high risk tolerance level, you can make some money by just buying bitcoin cheap in one country and selling it expensively in another. However, this form of trading can be quite risky when misjudged; you can lose money due to sudden changes in the market.

  Taking full advantage of the available technology will also help you gain maximum profits.

- Have a goal before entering any trade. A trade should only be started when you have a concrete reason to do so and have devised a clear strategy that will see you through. This will help you to determine when to cash in. You will stay focused, unemotional and more professional. Even if your aim is to trade daily, you may notice it makes more sense not to earn and do nothing than just rushing and losing your coins anyhow.

  Remaining professional will help you trade under no pressure. It ensures that you start trading only when you have the optimal conditions and are sure of when and how to get out of it. Remember, trading under pressure is tantamount to making major losses; avoid it completely. The next opportunity will just come and you will reap big.

- Always diversify your investment. Putting your 'eggs in one basket' is a very risky undertaking. Break down your capital into smaller lots and enter into multiple positions of different price levels.

- Avoid investing your life savings or money that may adversely affect your life, in case of losses. Remember, bitcoin market is still bridled with a lot of uncertainty.

- Risk management: It is unwise to look for the peak of the movement. Always look for small profits that potentially accumulate into a big one. Know how to manage risk well, especially over the wider investment portfolio. E.g., a non-liquid market (which is normally very risky) doesn't deserve an investment of more than small percentage of your portfolio.

- Don't be afraid to do test transactions. Normally, digital currencies are less stable compared to the conventional currencies. Therefore, before sending a transaction, find out if the other party has a secure wallet. You can begin by sending a small number of units and requesting that they be sent back to you. If the process turns out smoothly, you can be sure that the next transaction will be completed in a similar manner.

- Always choose your exchange or broker carefully. Get an exchange that is most reliable and flexible enough so that you are not inconvenienced in any way. If you opt for a platform that specializes in bitcoins, it will be much better.

- Avoid selling your bitcoin too soon. After investing, take some time, monitor your bitcoins and begin taking steps that will enable you make huge profits. However, don't hold onto it longer. You may miss the opportunity to make much more earnings. Also, consider selling only small amounts when you need the money, while retaining the rest in the network.

- You may be interested in maintaining your anonymity; this shouldn't trouble you that much. You can still buy bitcoins by mail through such a service as BitBrothers LLC. Though you'll pay a certain fee, this service will enable you to acquire bitcoins without necessarily logging in online.

- As a trader, always keep in mind that losing just like winning, is part of the game. In the long run, the cumulative gains will make you more proud than you think. Happy bitcoin trading!

The Future Of Bitcoin

Bitcoin's decentralized nature makes investors classify it as a fundamentally strong cryptocurrency. This description means that bitcoin has a longer and wider scope of growth. This perhaps explains why the price of bitcoin keeps gaining steadily while offering good profits to investors.

The decentralized nature has been catalytic and pivotal in revolutionizing commerce by enabling transactions to take place across international borders with a lot of ease. For instance, bitcoin allows you to send transactions for a fraction of the cost of most conventional payment platforms and owning a bitcoin wallet doesn't necessarily cost you anything in terms of account registration and maintenance.

It is quite apparent that bitcoin has many advantages. For this reason, it is likely to remain relevant for quite a long time. Below are some of the indicators that the future of bitcoin is bright:

- The continued acceptance of bitcoin on various trading platforms: An increasing number of larger corporations have begun offering bitcoin as an alternative payment method. This means that those companies that are still waiting in the shadows will eventually jump onto the bandwagon; a chain-reaction trigger that is likely to see bitcoin survive longer and even become a universal currency.

  Several colleges in the US have also begun accepting bitcoin as a means of payment, a move that is likely to be instrumental in bringing bitcoin to the mainstream as an alternative currency.

- Bitcoin's market capitalization (it currently has a market cap of over $160 billion) is somehow an indicator that this cryptocurrency has grown to be too big to collapse. Even though it is widely argued that bitcoin is currently in a speculative bubble, ascertaining when the bubble will collapse remains unclear. And even if the collapse were to happen, most players are still confident that bitcoin will most likely survive by a measure of its own self.

- Soon, we're likely to see the enablement of snap payments with bitcoins for Freelancers, Websites, Social Media enthusiasts, etc. As such, you will begin accepting any amount of bitcoins and immediately get it converted to USDs or Euros and avail it to your pre-paid Debit Card, by just inserting some simple codes on your website in order to accept the payment.

- Bitcoin will also be adopted in the much of the developed world, where there are no payment systems that allow instantaneous person-to-person payment. However, regulators in these countries may pose the biggest barrier to the growth of this cryptocurrency. Establishing local bitcoin exchanges to take care of the huge demand may also be an uphill task owing to the mixed reactions surrounding the acceptance of bitcoins.

Bitcoin as a protocol continues to evolve. Remember, bitcoin is a protocol first and the currency part happens to be the first app that was written over it. This means that more and more apps are being developed based on the bitcoin protocol, and may completely redefine the way online transactions are carried out in the future. For instance, the bitcoin currency may soon be dethroned and Litecoin or Dogecoin may prevail, thereby creating immense opportunities for investors. Just keep your eyes open and scout for such opportunities.

Indeed, many questions still abound as to whether bitcoin could be taken to be a 21st century version of gold or it is just a short-lived popular fad that is likely to evolve into something quite different in the near future. What remains clear is the fact that bitcoin continues to attract a wide appeal, particularly from a section of technology-savvy individuals, which will definitely be a big booster in its market performance, despite its volatility.

Conclusion

Bitcoin is an emerging technology that can revolutionize online transactions. By investing in bitcoin, you can keep your actions reasonably private from online predators while remaining in total control of your transactions. Therefore, now is the time to invest! Dive in and benefit from bitcoin's price volatility. Nevertheless, as you do, keep in mind that bitcoins and other cryptocurrencies are highly volatile and unregulated. You could lose your entire investment. Therefore, only invest what you can afford to lose!

If you found the book valuable, can you recommend it to others? One way to do that is to post a review on Amazon.

Part 3: Ethereum

An Essential Beginner's Guide to Ethereum Investing, Mining and Smart Contracts

Introduction

This book has actionable information about Ethereum that will help you to understand the ins and outs of investing, mining and smart contracts.

The rise of crypto-currencies and the subsequent popularity has brought with it the emergence of moneymaking opportunities that had never been witnessed before. Think about it: bitcoin, the leading crypto-currency, has increased in value by more than ten times in the last 4 years alone, from lows of $500 per bitcoin to over $5000 per bitcoin. With these high prices, bitcoins are increasingly going out of reach for the ordinary folk. The question is: Is there a way to make a killing off of crypto-currencies without having to invest so much to get bitcoins? Yes, there is, and Ethereum is the way to go.

Are you eager to create your own success story? Would you like to join a dynamic investment scheme, one that perfectly blends into your daily schedule (you don't really have to trade - you just buy, hold for some time then sell) and offers immense benefits? Then Ethereum may be all you need to make your dreams a reality. Indeed, Ethereum is an exciting revolutionary investment option that can guarantee a brighter financial future. Therefore, take advantage of it and start reaching for success.

This guide aims at expediting your discovery of smarter investment strategies by providing basic information about Ethereum to help you seamlessly build your investment portfolio, while confidently navigating the various concepts of mining and smart contracts and gaining attractive returns.

This guide is also fully aware that Ethereum is still in its infancy and is laced with unique risks and complexities. As such, your ingenuity is essential in devising new initiatives and innovative approaches that can help you navigate this fast-growing domain without being overwhelmed by the emerging pitfalls and barriers. However, like any other investment plan, always remember that hard work and consistency pays! So, let's plunge right into Ethereum!

Chapter 1: Ethereum: A Comprehensive Background

What is Ethereum?

Simply put, Ethereum refers to an open software platform that's founded on blockchain technology which provides developers with an opportunity to build and deploy applications from anywhere around the world.

For you to understand this definition better, let's first discus what blockchain technology entails.

Blockchain Technology

First and foremost, nowadays, most of our financial information, passwords and personal data are mainly stored on other people's computers and or servers owned by such companies as Google, Facebook, Netflix or Amazon. Thus, these companies deploy teams of highly skilled personnel that work tirelessly to help store and secure your data, regardless of what happens. This gives you a lot of convenience. For instance, you can easily access your data from any part of the world, as long as you've a reliable connection to the internet.

However, this convenience comes with a host of challenges. In some cases, the hosting company may charge you to hold your data when called upon and large volumes of data may attract hefty hosting charges. Also, when using such applications as Netflix or Facebook, you may encounter instances where a site is "down" and you can't move as fast as you would wish. This means that the application can't access the data it needs as a result of various impeding issues; and should the data center or server break down, then the application stops working completely. Quite nauseating, isn't it?

Additionally, your data is highly vulnerable and may succumb to threats from external attacks. Any government or a hacker can attack or influence the third party server, thereby gaining access to your data without your knowledge. With such unauthorized access, the hackers can even go as far as altering, leaking or stealing your important information.

Because of these shortcomings, decentralization of the internet has always been thought to be long overdue. In this regard, many tools are being devised to realize this goal. Blockchain technology is one of these tools. Blockchain technology was brought into the limelight by Satoshi Nakamoto in 2009 and continues to evolve as it grows in popularity. Max Kaplan, a blockchain enthusiast, defines a blockchain as a series of distributed computing devices that are linked to each other while sharing and authenticating data. A blockchain actually refers to a database that's distributed across multiple different computing devices placed anywhere around the world. These computing devices are also referred to as "nodes" and they share the same data. In simple terms, a blockchain is a kind of digital ledger which is shared among multiple computers. This means that if one node or computer malfunctions, it isn't a big deal since other nodes in the same chain have identical data.

Blockchain technology has essentially formed the backbone of a new type of internet. This is because it enables digital information to be distributed, but not replicated or reproduced, while using many computing devices - a fact that enhances its security ratings. The decentralized nature of blockchains makes hacking impossible since no one can gain direct access to tamper with your data.

Even though blockchain technology was originally invented for Bitcoin, the digital currency, tech enthusiasts continue to discover other uses associated with this technology. As such, it has become a trusted platform where many applications can be developed from. For instance, applications that require data security and multi-procedural validation, such as anti-money laundering schemes, find blockchains more appealing.

Bitcoin was the first popular application to employ the use of blockchains. Bitcoin's blockchain mainly acts as an irreversible financial ledger, thereby making it a more secure cryptocurrency. Cryptocurrency refers to a digital or virtual currency that employs the use of encryption techniques (commonly known as cryptography) in regulating the generation of currency units and the subsequent verification of the transfer of funds without the direct control of a central bank. Therefore, bitcoin is a type of cryptocurrency that's independent of any central bank's authority, relies on mathematical proof, and serves as an efficient but less expensive electronic payment system. The easiest way to describe a cryptocurrency is that it's not issued by a central bank or government authority and doesn't have a physical form, like a coin or a banknote.

The rapid worldwide acceptance of blockchain technology, and Bitcoin, is attributed to its unique qualities of transparency and incorruptibility. Actually, a blockchain network operates in a state of consensus in that it routinely checks in with itself after every ten minutes. Thus, the network automatically reconciles each and every transaction that takes place in intervals of ten minutes. Once transactions occur, they're recorded in "blocks" that are later entered into ledgers to be validated by a given number of computers within the respective blockchain network. Most importantly, the ledger occurs in the same form across the entire network.

Even though the user or the person performing a transaction may be anonymous, the trail of these blocks remains public and no one can alter any unit of information on it. Thus, anyone can gain access to the complete history of all transactions that take place and all changes are made visible to everyone as well. Generally, Bitcoin's strength lies in the fact that it increases efficiencies and eliminates the possibility of fraud by providing objective proof-of-work that guarantees security and validity in any transaction. And that's how Bitcoin remains a trusted option in digital transactions.

It is also important to note that, traditionally, digital transactions have demanded authorization or validation from third parties, such as banks. Indeed, this has been a very important step since money on a digital platform occurs as a file and can be copied and reused. However, involving such intermediaries comes at a cost since banks often make you play in their sandbox, and part with any amount of fees that is demanded. However, Bitcoin's use of digital signatures and public ledgers enables anonymous and secure transactions devoid of any trust to take place, because the public network of nodes authenticates transactions by ensuring that a majority of nodes must reach a unanimous agreement.

It's widely argued that Bitcoin has become adoptable in markets whose currencies are highly inflated and are in need of specific tools that can facilitate the deployment and exchange of currencies. Likewise, those markets with inadequate traditional financial infrastructure, but with sufficient mobile data, find Bitcoin more worthwhile and sustainable in carrying out various transactions.

Theoretically, cryptocurrencies can hardly ever suffer interference from authorities because only the person with the private key can access them and they're stored in no particular place whatsoever. Therefore, a government can't just seize them, since reaching most of the nodes may not be practical.

From the above explanation, you've definitely gained a clear idea of what blockchain technology entails. You've noticed the application of blockchains in cryptocurrency and seen how secure this platform is. Now we can go back to Etherium.

Etherium operates just like Bitcoin in that it relies on the broad strokes of a blockchain. It is an open network that's managed and controlled by its users without the interference of any bank or government. However, Etherium is not just a cryptocurrency (not just a digital currency), but contains other features that make it a stronger option for digital trade. In other words, Etherium functions as a platform through which individuals can make use of Ether tokens to create and operate, or run applications while exploiting its revolutionary feature of smart contracts. Before exploring these features further, let's have a look at some of the uses of Ethereum.

Uses of Ethereum

Using Ethereum gives you an added advantage of participating in the global computational network. In fact, blockchains make these uses possible. Some of the notable uses are:

- **Protection of intellectual property**: One of the drawbacks of being on the internet is that the internet allows for the infinite reproduction and distribution of digital information. As such, global web users can easily access a goldmine of free digital content, thereby disadvantaging genuine copyright holders who eventually lose control over their intellectual property and suffer financial loses as well.

  However, on Ethereum networks, copyright holders have a lot to smile about. You don't have to worry anymore as a copyright holder because you only have to use smart contracts to protect and automate the sale of your creative works and essentially remove the risk of reproduction and redistribution of your files. If you're an artist in the musical field, you can use the blockchain to establish the paternity of your work, define the terms of the smart contract through which granted licenses can be stipulated and executed, and protect it against unauthorized use.

  Moreover, open source objects can instantly and freely be patented by the blockchain because a patent simply involves a concept stamped and stored in a place where it can't be falsified. For instance, Mycelia, a UK peer-t0-peer distribution system for music, is based on Ethereum and provides a platform through which musicians can make direct sales to audiences, and producers can issue license samples while divvying up royalties to musicians and songwriters. In addition, Ascribe project was launched in 2014 with the aim of assisting creators in securing their intellectual property rights using blockchain technology. Any single kind of license, like Creative Commons licenses (CC), is admissible at Ascribe. So if you've any work, just record and register it under the CC license section on the blockchain as follows:

- Open the Ascribe's website by going to **http://cc.ascribe.io**

- Upload the work you intend to patent and fill in the appropriate metadata. Ensure the fields of title, author and year are correctly and accurately filled.

- Finally, click "Register" once you have selected CC license.

Once you've done that, the system will automatically register your file securely, ensuring that your file is stamped under the terms and conditions of license and all the metadata provided is included, on the blockchain. And with a Creative Commons License, you gain the real "smart contract," since you can keep track of your work over the traffic as well as the online reuse.

- **Stock trading**: Blockchains are good for stock trading due to the potential of enhanced efficiency in share settlement. This is because blockchain stock trading allows for instantaneous peer-to-peer execution, unlike in the traditional case where an allowance of a period of 3 days is inevitable for clearance to take place. This is a clear indication that traders can efficiently transact without involving such intermediaries as auditors, custodians and clearing house.

- **Land title registration**: The process of acquiring property titles has proved to be tedious and full of numerous besetting challenges. This is because such processes are labor intensive costly undertakings that are highly susceptible to fraud. But with blockchains, you're provided with publicly-accessible ledgers that make all the various kinds of record-keeping more efficient and well-organized. Most countries are drifting to undertaking land registry projects that are based on blockchain technology. Sweden, the Republic of Georgia and Honduras are some of the countries that are experimenting with the various blockchain applications for managing property titles.

- **Data management**: Currently, perhaps you're using social media platforms, such as Facebook, free of charge in exchange for your personal data. However, Ethereum can potentially give you an opportunity to conveniently manage and sell the data generated by your online activities. For instance, the MIT project Enigma has incorporated the tenets of user privacy as essential facets in the creation of a personal data marketplace. By using cryptographic techniques, Enigma allows individual sets of data to be shared between nodes while simultaneously running bulk computations over the whole data group. Also, Enigma allows for data fragmentation - a feature that makes it more scalable.

- **Anti-money laundering and Know your customer practices:** The daunting continuous labor intensive multi-step processes performed by financial institutions for each and every new customer can be a thing of the past by just adapting the blockchain technology. Blockchain technology will potentially reduce such costs by facilitating cross-institution client verification as well as enhancing the effectiveness of monitoring and analysis of transactions. For instance, Polycoin has anti-money laundering solutions that involve analyzing and singling out suspicious transactions to be forwarded for action by compliance officers.

- **Identity management**: The urgent need for a better identity management system on the web cannot be understated. Your ability to prove your identity is an essential component of your online financial transactions. But you may have noticed that mitigation measures for those security risks associated with web commerce are inadequate and may not guarantee a fair trade. This is because development of digital identity standards is a more complex endeavor than it appears. For example, getting the much-needed cooperation between the government and private sector as well as navigating the legal systems of different countries prove to be more challenging than envisaged. By involving the use of distributed ledgers in your online transactions, you can tap into a wealth of resources of verifying your identity and even get a controlled platform of digitizing your personal documents. E-commerce on the internet depends on the SSL certificate for secure transactions. Netki hopes to create an SSL standard for the blockchain and enhance the safety features of online transactions.

- **Supply chain auditing**: Customers are increasingly getting eager to ascertain whether ethical claims made by companies about their respective goods and services are genuine. The easiest and most efficient way to confirm that the backstories of the goods you purchase are real is to use distributed ledgers. The timestamping of a particular date and location, which corresponds to the number of the product courtesy of the blockchain, enhances transparency and can significantly contribute to customer loyalty. When integrated with the Internet of things (IoT), blockchain ensures products' real-time visibility, verification, inventory tracking, and their overall identity attestation. For instance, Provenance app —

which is based in the UK- is renowned for offering supply chain auditing for various consumer goods. For example, a Provenance pilot project that's based on the Ethereum blockchain ensures that fish is sustainably harvested by its Indonesian suppliers before being sold in Sushi restaurants in Japan.

- **Crowdfunding**: You may have heard of various crowdfunding initiatives such as Gofundme and Kickstarter. These initiatives continue to redefine the emerging peer-to-peer economy, probably due to the fact that most people desire to have a direct say in the development of various products. You could use the Ethereum network to take this interest to another level and potentially create venture capital funds that are crowd-sourced.

For instance, just look for a unique idea that you can develop on Ethereum. The idea may be so involving that you need help and some funds to actualize and bring it to life. At this juncture, you don't need to worry and get overwhelmed with the immense assignment that lies ahead. Just use Ethereum and create a contract that can hold the money from your donors until the specified date or when you achieve your intended objective. Ethereum's safety features will ensure that the funds collected are reimbursed to the donors or just released to the owners of the project. Again, donors can use your tokens (Ether tokens) to monitor how rewards are being distributed. These transactions can take place without the need for trust, or any centralized arbiter.

- **File storage**: As noted earlier on, what makes blockchains more revolutionary is the fact that data is distributed throughout the network. You're most likely to find this nature of decentralizing the storage of files more beneficial than just using ordinary servers. Notably, your files are automatically protected from any external threats and you won't encounter any points of failure whenever you want to access your data. Further, with completely decentralized websites, the internet potentially speeds up the times for streaming and file transfer. Certainly, this is a much-needed improvement since it conveniently serves as an essential upgrade to the current methods of delivering content on the web, which are overloaded.

- **The sharing economy**: The flourishing of such companies as AirBnB and Uber gives a clear testimony that the concept of the sharing economy is a success. But you must depend on an intermediary like Uber if you are eager to hail a ride-sharing service. Therefore, the blockchain potentially paves way for direct interactions between different parties, through its ability to provide an avenue for peer-to-peer payments. A good case in point is the OpenBazaar app, which uses the blockchain technology to set up a peer-to-peer eBay. You can download the OpenBazaar app and start transacting with its vendors without incurring transaction costs. Furthermore, the protocol has a "no rules" ethos, which ensures that personal reputation has a higher weighting in business interactions than the current case on eBay and other online trading companies.

- **Governance**: Ethereum's distributed database technology can enhance transparency in any electoral process across the globe, through its salient feature of making the voting process and ensuing results totally transparent and publicly accessible. The processes of identity verification, voter registration and the subsequent ledger protection of the votes can efficiently ensure the entire electoral process is as tamperproof as possible.

Similarly, suppose you want to hire managers in your organization, do a bunch of paperwork or run some board meetings, then Ethereum contracts can collect proposals from your backers and present them in a manner that the voting process is completely transparent to enable you make wise decisions. Also, by employing the use of the Boardroom app, your organizational decision-making processes can take place on blockchain using the Business Logic Coding model. This means that the processes of managing your company's information, equity or digital assets will be more transparent and verifiable, even though multiple stages of approval may have been eliminated, thereby ensuring fluent and better dispute resolution mechanisms.

- **Prediction markets**: You must have noticed that crowdsourced predictions on event probability have a higher level of accuracy. This is because you get an added advantage of cancelling out your unexamined biases that may have distorted your judgment by averaging opinions from different sections of the population.

With blockchains, you can easily source for opinions from different individuals and make accurate predictions. You can access many apps online, especially those that make share offerings on the aftermath of events in the real-world, and begin earning money by just buying into the right prediction. By purchasing more shares in the correct outcome, you'll definitely get a higher payout irrespective of your initial capital.

You can commit even a small amount of funds, say even less than a dollar, formulate a question, ask it, and come up with a market that's dependent on a predicted outcome. This will offer you an opportunity to collect half of all transaction fees generated by the market, and you can increase your earnings by continually learning how to tailor your questions to match current events and real-life situations. Besides, if you're a fan of betting, you can benefit from "BetHite," a smart contract-based betting product, and you may potentially revolutionize the gamut of peer-to-peer betting in sports and other related events.

- **Neighborhood micro grids**: You can certainly buy and sell renewable energy generated by the microgrids in your neighborhood. Once your solar panels produce excess energy, you can automatically redistribute it using smart contracts on the Ethereum network. For instance, Consensys company, which develops a range of applications for Ethereum, has partnered and implemented the Transactive Grid project that uses Ethereum smart contracts to automate how microgrid energy is redistributed among various users.

- **Internet of Things**: This refers to the network-controlled management of particular kinds of electronic devices, like monitoring the air temperature in a given storage facility. The automation of the management of remote systems is made possible by employing the use of smart contracts. The combined interaction and linkages between the network, sensors and the software enables data exchanges between mechanisms and objects, consequently increasing the efficiency of the system, as well as improving cost monitoring practices.

- **Medical records**: Blockchain enables you to secure your patient's personal information using private keys. And if you're a tech guru, you can also encode health records and store them securely on blockchain. Thus, using blockchains can definitely improve the credibility and authenticity of healthcare, as well as the insurance industry at large. In a nutshell, some of the blockchain healthcare uses are:

- Pharmacy tracing and tracking
- Reinforcing of secure mobile and remote sharing system innovations
- Carrying out payments
- Keeping track of medical records

There are numerous blockchain healthcare related companies that can be beneficial to you. One of these companies is MedRec, which manages medical records through blockchain. MedRec will give you census-level data of your health records, and the data is often obtained in the form of both research and clinical blockchain. Invented by MIT graduate student researchers, MedRec's novel design feature lies in how records are validated before being added to the blockchain. Medical researchers are the miners for MedRec and accessing the medical records' census-level data is the miners' reward. Once a MedRec system is deployed, a user interface is incorporated to simplify the way patients interact with medical records, bridging several institutions.

Ethereum is still evolving and many applications are being discovered day by day. This means that investment opportunities continue to evolve as well, and you can pick an area of your interest and explore it further.

Different startups are experimenting with various apps to meet as many uses as possible on the Ethereum network. This is a clear indication that even if you're least grounded in programming and coding, or you don't have time to work out complex mathematical problems and develop various apps on Ethereum network, you can still make money by just running those apps that've already been developed.

Enrolling for some of the Ethereum classes will also sharpen your skills and build your confidence on how to maneuver emerging challenges. As such, it's important to explore Ethereum's unique selling prepositions in order to have an idea of what to get whenever you delve into it. As noted earlier on, Ethereum's unique features lie in its smart contracts and the Ether. Let's have a look at what encompasses these features.

Smart Contracts

Ethereum's smart contracts refer to indisputable digitally controlled exchange mechanisms that potentially facilitate direct value transactions between untrusted parties or agents. A smart contract involves any contract written in code and uploaded to the blockchain by the creator. Smart contracts are essential in verifying, facilitating, or enforcing the performance or negotiation of technical commands that are economically laden as well as avoiding counter-party risk, collusion, incidences of downtime, and censorship. Ideally, a smart contract digitally overseas the exchange of anything of value, such as shares, property, content, or money, by clearly defining the rules and penalties around the agreement as well as ensuring that those obligations are automatically enforced. Smart contracts can be described as self-operating computer programs meant to be automatically implemented whenever specific conditions are met.

For example, suppose you want to buy a house a house from your realtor. You can conveniently do this on blockchain by paying through cryptocurrency. You'll get a receipt, which is subsequently held in your virtual agreement. Your realtor will also give you the digital entry key, which must reach you by the specified date. If you can't get the key on time, the blockchain will automatically release a refund to you. Also, if your realtor sends the key before the date of purchase, the system will first hold it and release the key to you and the fee to your realtor on the due date. Smart contracts are witnessed by many people and they work on the premise of If – then to guarantee safe transactions. In this case, you're sure to get the house once you make the requisite payment. So, you can use smart contracts to perform as many transactions as possible.

Once you code your smart contract and upload it on the blockchain, it becomes a decentralized application, or an autonomous script, that is stored for later implementation by the Ethereum Virtual Machine (EVM). We shall discuss EVM further later. The important point to note is that Ethereum smart contracts are instrumental in adopting a conflict free way of carrying out online transactions since they give birth to more efficient and streamlined processes that are devoid of any human intervention. With smart contracts, you don't need any authority or agent to secure and guarantee the honesty of the transaction, rather the system itself does this for you.

How smart contracts work

Before moving further, perhaps you're wondering how exactly smart contracts translate to earnings. This isn't as complex as you think. especially if you're not all that into the technical stuff behind the Ethereum network.

According to Wikipedia, the commands entrenched in Ethereum's smart contracts are paid for in Ether. Ether basically refers to energy or the "gas" that runs the Ethereum network. In simple terms, Ether can be defined as a virtual currency that's employed in paying for the implementation of the Ethereum's smart contracts, a process that consumes significant resources. So, as a volunteer, you can earn the Ether by validating transactions while keeping the entire network as secure as possible.

Technically, smart contracts rely on a computer coding system that's smart and advanced. The resulting computer programs may formerly encode definite conditions and consequences, in which the codes involved are based on prior consensuses of the contracting parties. Turing-complete is the language used by Ethereum to allow developers to create their own programs since it supports a broader set of computational commands. An example of the Turing-complete language is solidity. These tutorials can help you learn how to use the language. Basically, smart contracts potential lie in:

- Functioning as "multi-signature accounts" in which the expenditure of funds is only permitted whenever a certain percentage of people agree.

- Managing users' agreements.

- Provision of utility to other contracts. This means that smart contracts may need assistance from other smart contracts in order to function. This sounds complex, isn't it? Consider this example: Suppose your friend places a bet on a cold winter day, it eventually triggers a sequence of related contracts. They'll need a contract that may employ the use of data from outside to determine the weather, while another contract would be used to settle the bet depending on the information received from the initial contract as long as the conditions are duly satisfied.

- Storing any information about the application, like records of members or information about domain registration.

Theoretically, smart contracts operate in the following manner:

- Contract terms must first be translated into computer code: The idea is to have a deterministic digital system. Therefore, all issues related to the contract like resolution of disputes or breach of contract must be clearly stipulated.

- The parties must agree on which code to use.

- The code must be run in a fair manner.

Isn't this very exciting? Come on, think of any problem to solve, come up with a contract, upload it on the Ethereum platform and begin to earn some dollars! As a beginner, you may find the greeter resourceful.

Using Ethereum smart contracts offers many opportunities that can make businesses more efficient and profitable. In particular, Ethereum contracts eliminate the need to have third parties for validation and authentication of your contracts, safeguards your business from external manipulation of your contract terms, ensures immutability and ensures automation of tasks as well as cost effective and more accurate processes. Also, Ethereum smart contracts make sure that your business information is saved multiple times and can be easily accessed by blockchain users as long as they have private keys. This allows for convenient access to information as well as its authentic verification by consensus.

Even though smart contracts appear to be the game changer in online transactions, they're still being received with some level of skepticism across the globe. The main suspicion around the use of the smart contracts stems from the fact that there's the absence of legislation concerning the enforceability of the titles recorded on blockchain. Moreover, it's not possible for authorities to intervene or repress any party just in case illicit activities are carried out through smart contracts. Thus, the challenges of relying on Ethereum's smart contracts are hinged on their underlying cryptographic technology that's largely opaque for most legal processes. Also, the use of smart contracts on a public blockchain means that bugs, such as security holes, can't be fixed easily, despite the fact that they're visible to all.

The Ether

Ether simply refers to Ethereum blockchain's value token that is listed under ETH code and traded on various cryptocurrency exchanges. Ether is used to settle payments for computational services as well as transaction fees on the Ethereum network and it can also be traded easily for fiat currencies like Euros or dollars. In as much as Ether functions as any other currency, just like Bitcoin or even dollars, Ether is also the fuel that runs the Ethereum network. When you complete a transaction, you'll be paid in the form of gas. The process of data verification on the blockchain is powered by this gas. Gas represents the miners' fee.

Miners perform expensive and energy intensive activities of processing transactions and keeping the Ethereum network secure. Particularly, gas gives a measure of the complexity of an operation. Thus, if an operation is more complex, then it costs more gas. For instance, if you add two numbers, it'll cost you 3 gas, while multiplying 2 numbers costs you 5 gas, since such an operation is more complex. Gwei, a denomination currency smaller than Ether, is what is used to measure the price of gas. 1 billion Gwei make one Ether.

Therefore, when developing smart contracts, you must make the code as simple as possible to reduce on gas costs and encourage users to interact with your application. Please note that Ether tokens are known to suffer market volatility. This is because unlike a Bitcoin transaction, which takes 10 minutes, Ether transactions last 15 seconds, resulting in its liquidity and volatility. And as many people get interested in Ethereum, its value continues to rise and a single transaction, which is marked by a large sell order, may lead to significant changes in its value.

Ether's liquidity allows for swift conversion to and from fiat currencies. Still, the supply of Ether is infinite and is driven by its creators and miners. Technologists predict that Ethereum's value will only stabilize once it achieves its objective of being a globally decentralized platform that allows interactions between humans and billions of devices. Ether may experience great highs and lows, due to the frequent in and out movements of investors, but the long run price is expected to be considerably bigger than the current one.

It's also important to note that Ether's launch was characterized by crowdfunding and, as a result, most of the people who purchased this currency own it. Experts predict that the balance is likely to shift in the favor of the Ether miners in the forthcoming five years. And as you begin to invest, always remember that Ethereum and Ethereum Classic are different in order to avoid falling prey to fraudulent schemes. Ethereum Classic (ETH) is basically an unofficial spin-off run by people who are not part of the actual Ethereum Project team.

Ethereum Virtual Machine (EVM)

EVM refers to the completely isolated and sandboxed runtime environment for Ethereum's smart contracts. The codes that run inside the EVM can't access file systems, network or other processes. The environment is made in such a way that even smart contracts have limited access to others.

An EVM code is comprised of a series of bytes, with each and every byte representing a given operation. This composition likens an EVM code to a stack based bytecode language. An infinite loop characterizes the code's execution with the output being a byte array of data.

EVM is a Turing-complete software and can enable any developer to run any program, irrespective of the language of programming used, as long as there's sufficient time and memory. With the Ethereum Virtual Machine, the process of creating blockchain applications is more efficient and easier than it was before. Therefore, thousands of different applications can be potentially developed on the Ethereum platform.

Other remarkable features that make Ethereum valuable are:

- Sovereignty: For a transaction on Ethereum to be valued, your balance must be greater than the amount you're sending, regardless of the purpose for which you're sending or receiving the funds. Also, as an Ethereum network user, you're free to decide how to spend your funds without any authorization. You'll find this more beneficial during those tough times when the country may be experiencing wanton cases of money controls and hyperinflation, because you're able to untether from the fiat currency system.

- Mathematics and scarcity: As seen earlier on, the laws of Mathematics drive the Ethereum blockchain. The distribution of Ethereum's currency is immutably coded, publicly available and arrived at after a consensus agreement.

Having had a brief overview of the various features of Ethereum network and gaining confidence in how cryptocurrencies operate, now you can go further and start investing in Etherium. The next chapter looks at investing in Ethereum to enable you take ownership of the process and make informed choices from the available options.

Chapter 2: Investing in Ethereum

You can buy Ethereum at any Ethereum Exchange. After buying the Ether, you can store the funds in your own secure wallet or on the exchange itself. Storage on the exchange is most appropriate when you're dealing with small purchases of Ethereum because you can easily access your funds. However, if you're considering making large purchases of Ethereum, then you better move your funds to your own secure wallet. Before going into particular steps of Ethereum investment, let's define some terms that you'll encounter in the course of your transactions.

- **Ethereum miner**: This is a machine that compiles transactions into blocks before slotting them into the blockchain. The miner must successfully complete difficult computational problems before adding blocks to the blockchain.

- **Ethereum node**: This involves any computational device that contains a complete copy of the Ethereum blockchain. A group of thousands of nodes, each confirming and validating each and every transaction on the blockchain, constitute the Ethereum network.

- **Exchange:** This is a platform from which you can buy and sell cryptoassets. Always do your research well in order to get a good exchange, i.e. one that has a good reputation and perfectly suits your needs. The exchange you choose will depend on such factors as your personal preference, your place or area of residence, and the various laws that govern cryptocurrency trading. Remember, you will be required to sign up and even provide some proof of identification before trading on some of these exchanges. Conversely, you don't necessarily have to sign up for an account on other exchanges, like ShapeShift and Changelly, although such cases mostly apply when you already have other currencies that you would like to convert to Ether. As a result, you won't be required to provide your personal information, automatically doing away with the urge to remember passwords.

- **Market cap:** This refers to the product of total value of the supply of coin and the price of each coin. Market cap may be used to estimate the value of the entire network.

- **Fiat currency**: This refers to any legal tender - it could be British Pounds, Euros or US dollars, for example.

- **Cryptoasset**: This refers to any asset that's secured by cryptography, mostly those assets that are based on blockchain like Bitcoin or Ethereum.

- **Ethereum token**: Remember Ethereum's main goal is to provide a platform for creating decentralized applications (DAPPS). Once applications are built on top of the Ethereum, they can essentially create currencies of their own. Such currencies are referred to as Ethereum tokens and are poised to become a major component in the trading landscape of the cryptocurrency. In the long run, you will discover that anyone can create a token, which is good news since you can simply bolt on a token on your existing application and utilize it to begin raising funds. However, always be careful before considering investments in such tokens, since some of them may not be meant for genuine purposes and you could eventually lose your investment.

- **Private key**: You will be required to have an Ethereum wallet in order to transact on the Ethereum platform. The Ethereum wallet comes with a private key. This private key simply refers to your wallet's key. You must keep it as secret as possible. If anyone else gets your private key, it means they automatically get full access to your wallet and the funds therein. As you create your wallet, you'll be required to generate a copy of your private key. A private key is normally generated offline in most wallets, and it's hardly ever sent to a server to avoid being intercepted by third parties. Always back up and safely store your private key, because if you lose it, you automatically lose your funds.

The following reasons can motivate you to invest in Ethereum:

- You can buy Ethereum for use: This may involve paying wages internationally, operating smart contracts, interacting with the Internet of things devices that are based on blockchain, etc.

- You can just buy Ethereum for investment: In this case, you're able to diversify your traditional investment portfolio, hedge yourself against the current fiat system, or access blockchain investments such as token sales, etc.

Just like in any other investment scheme, it's prudent to have an investment strategy while plunging into Ethereum. You must objectively evaluate your own level of personal risk tolerance before making any move. Consulting a financial advisor may be a good idea, so that you're well acquainted with issues to do with market volatility and emerging trends in the industry. Some of the points to consider while strategizing are:

- Practice buying and holding: This strategy appears to be the trend on Ethereum network. The driving force behind this strategy is the firm belief that even if Ethereum was to replace just a fraction of any fiat currency, it will be of far greater value than it is at the moment. Furthermore, the same is likely to be the case if Ethereum is widely adopted as the only cryptocurrency for "machine payable web" and enable a wide array of devices to carry out efficient value transactions with each other.

  Due to the volatility of the Ether, it's recommended that you consider the concept of "dollar cost averaging." Try to spend your total investment amount while apportioning it over a given period of time so that you can buy the Ether at an average price. Just be wise and buy more when prices are low to compensate for the fewer you bought or are likely to buy at high prices. After buying, ensure that you store your Ether safely. Storing Ether in online wallets, exchanges, computer wallets, or mobile apps is not safe in the long run. You can use the following options for long term storage of Ether:

  o Ether paper wallets: Paper wallets aren't vulnerable to online hacking because you'll store them in any off-site location that's safe and accessible to you only, such as a safety deposit box, etc. Once stored there, any failure in computing devices won't bother you anymore. However, you must be careful since your password can leak to other people while you're creating your paper wallet. Also, you shouldn't lose your paper wallet, as this essentially means that your money is completely lost. You can follow the following steps to create your paper wallet:

- Look for a "dumb" laser-printer. As a security precaution, your printer should have USB connectivity and a very small memory capacity. Remember, a hacker can steal your password by intercepting it from a WIFI transmission or from the printer's memory. Let our printer be as simple as possible. Also, don't buy an inkjet printer so that the ink doesn't smear in wet environments.

- Get waterproof paper, especially one that is specifically suited for laser printers. Such a paper is also tear-proof. You don't want to lose your funds because your paper wallet got wet.

- Once you're online, create your first wallet using a wallet generator. You can go offline once you get your first wallet address. Before printing out the wallet, ensure you've generated a new address. Again, this is a cautious step because the website can transmit the information of the wallet to a hacker.

- Print out your wallet, ensuring a new wallet is generated every time. You may have to make several attempts to figure out how to properly align the front and the back. Printing your wallets to PDF and storing them on an encrypted flash drive is also a good idea. However, always keep in mind that having many backups increases the chances of someone stealing your Ether.

- Lastly, hide the private key by folding up the paper wallet. The private key is the password that permits you to spend your funds in the wallet, therefore, you must protect it.

- Depending on your level of sophistication, you may get tamper evident seals in order to tell whether someone has been peeping at your private key or not.

Once you've transferred your currency on the paper, ensure the paper is stored in a safe place. You can just use your mobile wallet app or an online wallet whenever you want to get your funds from the paper to your bank or your exchange of choice.

o Hardware wallets: Trezor is one of the hardware wallets that you can use. This can't be hacked, whether online or offline. It provides you with an opportunity to back up your wallet and restore them whenever you lose your device. It is easy to use, very durable, water-resistant and can simultaneously store multiple cryptocurrencies. But you must take care - ensure that no one gets your recovery card because your pin can be reset. Also, Trezor is likely to suffer all the vulnerabilities of any other electronic device and by storing all your Ether in one place you make it easy for anyone who has your PIN to steal from you.

A combination of hardware wallet and paper wallet is the best way to achieve a perfect blend of holding and buying. But you can choose an option that works best for you.

- Buying and diversifying: As a beginner, you may find this strategy very applicable since you can't predict the future of Ethereum. Even though Ethereum isn't likely to disappear soon, a little-known cryptoasset may just become dominant within a short period of time and cost you immensely. Therefore, you may consider purchasing Ethereum and swapping for other cryptoassets such as Ethereum Classic (ETC) and Ripple (XRP) to help you hedge against any unforeseen failure in the performance of any coin, especially if your investment is more than 400USD. Remember Ethereum has overtaken Bitcoin, probably because of its Smart contracts feature, so another innovation may also spring up and outdo Ethereum. The important point to consider is that while one coin may fail, the widely futuristic view is that cryptoassets of some kind may become ubiquitous. In diversifying your investment, you could adopt such a plan as:

  o Invest 10% in gambling stake: This can comprise of totally high-risk tokens.

  o Invest 30% in a stake that's risky but interesting: This should be coins that you foresee can experience some growth in the near future. Investing in tokens that have a market cap of less than $300 million may be a good idea.

  o Invest 60% in a safe stake: Your safe stake must be Ethereum since it's a no-brainer. You can refer to Ether as safe because it potentially portrays a moderate stability and a clear upward trend.

With diversification, ensure that you keep updating yourself on the market trends. You may discover that an investment that was good a month ago might not be that appealing at the moment. Therefore, stay informed in order to react as swiftly as possible. You may subscribe to credible weekly newsletters where real-time market analysis takes place. You may sign up for one here.

- Ethereum trading: This venture isn't for the faint-hearted as it involves compounding risk on an asset that's already volatile. But remember, risky undertakings are the ones that are laden with huge profits. If you feel you've enough muscle to withstand the shock, then try to day trade cryptoassets on various exchanges like GDAX and Poloniex. Just ensure your exchange gives you the ability to set different pending orders as well as stop losses. If your exchange doesn't give you those options, then you must set up alerts to enable you be on top of market movements and trade manually. Pro plan is the only exchange that provides alerts.

Use TradingView to set up alerts, and it's recommended that you become an active trader in order to benefit more. First search for the ETHUSD currency pair in the search box before adding it to your watchlist and clicking on it for the chat to pop up. Afterwards, right- click on the chart where an alert is to be added. For instance, suppose you want to add an alert close to the latest high, say near $400, since you're interested in selling your long position. You may include another alert to inform you whenever there are low prices and it might be the right time to buy.

Investing in Ethereum requires you to have a digital wallet. Please note that Ethereum trading isn't available on the major stock platforms. And as you invest, always remember that Ether (ETH) is a currency. In other words, with Ether, you don't buy shares like ETFs or any other stock. In actual fact, your investment means that you are simply exchanging your funds in fiat currency, say US dollars, for Ether tokens; your investment will not attract dividends or any payouts. However, your main motivation is the fact that in the future, other individuals on the internet will buy your Ether tokens at a higher price than the one you bought them at.

The Ether Wallet

So, before buying Ether, you need to familiarize yourself with the wallet software and the online transactions in general. This is because majorities of the cryptoassets have strict operational rules and procedures that can become extremely unforgiving at times. If you just make any slight false move when receiving or sending a transaction, you are likely to lose an entire bankroll or even lose your credibility on the entire network. This is the same case with Ethereum.

Furthermore, just like any other ordinary wallet, your Ethereum wallet can also be "stolen." Your Ethereum wallet risks being hacked if you leave it stored on a device that's connected to the internet most of the time. Remember, you can't recover a stolen wallet. No court can help you recover it, and reversing any accidental transaction isn't possible. Therefore, try to understand a bit of the technology behind Ethereum wallet and always exercise caution whenever you undertake your transactions.

That piece of software that stores or holds your Ether funds and other Ethereum-based tokens is what is called an Ethereum wallet. Ethereum wallets occur in the form of hardware/paper wallets, a mobile/web app, a desktop application, or any other online exchange. You can download the authorized Ethereum wallet from Ethereum.org. Once you open this website, especially as a new user, it's recommended that you download the "Light Client" option and not the "full node" one. With a "full node", you will also be required to download the full Ethereum blockchain, which is very heavy, in order to use it as a wallet. This is quite tedious. However, with a "Light client" you don't have to worry about getting the full blockchain in order for it to operate.

Sometimes, the Ethereum website may be a bit challenging to navigate through. As such, other websites have been created to enable traders to interact with the main Ethereum website. We will use one of these websites, myetherwallet.com, to create an Ethereum wallet. MyEtherWallet is a static web page, in order to try and minimize security risks. But you must download the website yourself, in order to minimize the risk of accessing a wrong page. By downloading the website, you'll also be able to use MyEtherWallet even when you're not connected to the internet. The following steps can get you started:

- Download the latest version of the MyEtherWallet **website**. It is a zip file, but make sure it is the "etherwallet-v…" and not the chrome extension. By unzipping the file, a list of website files will appear.

- Launch MyEtherWallet by double clicking on "index.html."

- Now, you're ready to create your password-protected Ethereum wallet. No one will ever be able to accidentally duplicate this password. (As a matter of fact, the number of Ethereum wallets is more than that of atoms in the universe.) At this point, turn off your internet connection before proceeding. To enhance your online safety, you may use a computer that's rarely or never connected to the internet. Such a computer is commonly considered to be an "air-gapped" computer. This is a good precautionary measure since it will help you minimize the risk that someone may have hacked into your computer and continues to remotely monitor your online activities.

- Create your new wallet. Think of a secure password that you can't forget and type it in the box. Then click on "Create New Wallet".

- You will then be prompted to click on "Download Keystore File." This process helps you save your wallet.

Get an encrypted USB stick and save it there. Your USB stick shouldn't hang around on your computer to avert any risk of being stolen. The file generated will be bearing such a name as "UTC—2017–08–11T15–29–26.452Z—45…". Click on "I understand. Continue" to go on with the process. Once the next page is opened, you'll see a plain text containing your "private key." This is simply a plain text version of the keystore file you downloaded and you don't have to save it since you already have it. Your "private key" is not password protected.

- This is optional. You may print a "paper wallet," which is basically a paper version of the keystore file that you already saved. This is meant to protect you just in case you forget your password or lose your keystore file. Once you print it, please store it safely because if the paper wallet is accessed by anyone, then you'll definitely lose your Ethereum.

- Then click on "See my address."

- Next, you can move on to confirm your balance after unlocking your wallet.

Just click on "View Wallet Info" tab, followed by "Select Wallet File." Remember your keystore file "UTC—2017–08–11…" that you had saved earlier on? You can click on "Unlock" after typing your keystore password.

After unlocking, you should be able to optionally display private key, transaction history links, your Ether balance, your public address, like

"0x45cABda7D6A2051dc7e20Cfc6d0bd4878f7D3736," and even print your paper wallet. Do not give out your private key. However, share your Account Address so that you can receive Ether.

- Your Token Balances are also visible on the side. These will generally appear as ERC20 tokens and represent BAT and AIR that you can also store in your Ethereum wallet.

You can click on "Show All Tokens" to reveal the balances of your individual token. At this point, you can now start trading!

- Start by receiving Ether. Nothing really special needed here! You only need to share the public address of your Ethereum wallet ("0x45cABda7D6A2051dc7e20Cfc6d0bd4878f7D3736") with the person you intend to receive Ether from. You can click "View Wallet Info" to check your Ether balance.

You can also receive Ether by buying it from your exchange. After buying Ethereum, your exchange's withdrawal function normally requests the address of your wallet. You can then input your address as well as the amount of Ether that you would like to withdraw to your wallet. After system confirmation, you'll be shown a transaction hash. You'll see your Ether in your wallet as "pending" straightaway, and you can use Etherscan.io to follow its number of confirmations.

There are many ways for buying Ethereum. We will explore them later.

- You may send Ether as well. You can send Ether whether you're online or not. But it's safer to use your wallet offline because you can reduce the potential of hackers stealing your wallet. To send Ether while still online, just unlock your wallet after clicking on "Send Ether & Tokens" tab.

- After unlocking, a page showing "To Address," amount, and gas limit will show up. And in case your wallet contains other ERC20 tokens, just click the ETH down arrow to change to the currency of your choice. The "Gas limit" refers to the maximum fee that you'll be charged by the network to execute your transaction. Remember that individual nodes, which represent people from different parts of the world voluntarily participating in the irksome processing work of the network, power the Ethereum network. Therefore, you pay them a fee to enable them process your transaction. Let the default 21000, which attracts 5 to 30 cents USD as a transaction fee. Normally, the system automatically sets the gas limit; however, always double check the cost, because miscalculations are bound to occur. It is also not necessary to specify the "from address" since this address will be selected automatically based on the balance that each address contains.

A transaction hash will be created and displayed to you on your screen, once you send your Ether transaction. By putting this transaction hash in a block explorer, you can also access the same details, as those displayed on your screen, of your new transaction.

Still, your Ethereum wallet will automatically create a number of receiving addresses. These receiving addresses are also referred to as public keys and are normally a function of your private key. Again, you are at liberty to share receiving addresses without risking theft, unlike your private key, and any payment to these receiving addresses will also add Ether to your wallet.

- Sending an offline transaction is pretty much the same. You just won't be able to execute the transaction until you are online. By sending an offline transaction, you can safely remove your keystore from the computer (by simply unplugging your USB) and prevent it from ever getting connected to the internet.

- While on the "Send Offline" tab, copy the address of your Ethereum wallet in the "From Address" field, before clicking on "Generate Information."

- Then, enter the Ethereum address that you want to send Ether tokens to, before filling in the type and the value. You can let the Gas Limit and Gas Price values remain in the default values.

- Now, select your keystore file and enter your password to unlock it. Proceed with clicking on "Generate Transaction".

- Finally, copy the text, "Signed Transaction," and transfer this transaction to a different computer to complete it. Or, just you may still use the same computer by connecting it to the internet, but you must remove your keystore (which is your real wallet) before starting to execute the transaction. This is a security measure that you have to take in order to ensure that your wallet isn't connected to the internet.

So, now that you're already armed with your wallet you can move forward and buy Ethereum.

Buying Ethereum

Since Ethereum is relatively young, you are not likely to come across many vendors selling it. As a result, buying Ethereum may not be easy, especially for a beginner. First and foremost, let's look at some of the vendors and exchanges from where you can buy Ether.

- Coinbase: This is considered to be the cheapest and most convenient way of buying and selling Ethereum and you can buy Ethereum using your debit or credit card. Coinbase sells Ether at a fee of between 1.49% and 3.99%, depending on your preferred method of payment. It can also allow you to buy Ether using your bank account, especially if you are living in the UK, USA, Singapore and Canada. In the US, buying with a bank account will take at least 7 days because the ACH banking system takes a bit of time to process transactions. But the process takes less than 2 days in Canada, the UK and Europe, especially if you are using SEPA transfer to deposit to your account. Coinbase takes you through a verification process and if you make purchases of above $100, you will automatically receive a bonus of $10. A minimum deposit of $1 is required at Coinbase. Please note that Coinbase also prides itself to be the only US regulated site that has insurance on funds, up to $250,000, and a proven track record.

- CEX.IO: This is a cloud mining site that was established in 2013. At the moment, it doubles as a cryptocurrency and it specializes on Ether tokens and Bitcoin. You can use payment cards, like virtual credit cards such as Payoneer and NetSpend, and bank transfers to buy Ether from CEX.IO. Cryptocurrency deposits attract no fee, while a $10 or 3.5%+$0.25 fee is charged on bank transfers and credit cards respectively. Also, keep in mind that you will be required to pay a 0.2% for subsequent transactions. The good news is that CEX.IO is found worldwide.

- Coinmama: This is a user-friendly website that specializes in selling Ether and Bitcoins. You can buy Ether on this website using Western Union money transfers and credit cards.

- BitPanda: This is the most fully automated platform meant for the purchase of Ether and Bitcoins. BitPanda supports most convenient payment methods, like PayPal, bank transfer, and cards. You'll need a minimum deposit of $25 and you'll find this platform very easy to navigate as a beginner.

- EXMO: This is also another trusted online cryptocurrency exchange from where you can buy Ethereum using a myriad of payment systems such as Bitcoin, bank transfers and credit cards.

- Alfacashier: You can use this if you're whacky about trying out a convenient online currency exchanger that offers multiple exchange directions. It allows perfect money, Bitcoin and SWIFT/SEPA transfer modes of payment.

- Localethereum: If you're interested in trading on anonymous market places, then this platform is best for you. Localethereum facilitates the buying and selling of Ether using smart contracts. It was launched on October 20th, 2017 and can enable you buy Ethereum from any place around the world. It accepts payments in form of cash, PayPal, bank transfer, and even cryptocurrency. However, you need a minimum deposit of $1 and you may find it a bit tedious to navigate as a beginner.

Other exchanges include: Gemini, Bitfinex, Kraken, GDAX, eToro, Poloniex, and BTC-e. The payment method you use to buy Ethereum will depend on your goals and even convenience. For instance, if you're interested in using a method that attracts low fees, then a bank transfer will work well for you. However, be prepared to wait longer before your transaction can be completed. But if you're conscious about your privacy, then you may first consider buying Bitcoins privately before approaching your exchange to buy Ether. And if in a hurry, then trying a credit card will be the most appropriate option for you.

All in all, you may find that the process of buying Ethereum varies from one exchange to another, however, it is simple and is characterized by certain fundamental principles that take the form of:

- Registering at an exchange of choice: You will be required to submit some of your personal details. Full identity checks will also be involved, especially whenever you make any deposit or perform withdrawal transactions.

- Completing identity or know your customer (KYC) checks: Your exchange will always carry out KYC and Anti-Money Laundering (AML) checks before or after depositing or prior to performing any withdrawal. Thus, you will be required to verify your account in a number of ways. For instance, you may have to provide proof of address as well as photo identification. Also, your account will have to pass a regulatory muster before proceeding with your transactions. The process of verification normally lasts between 1 and 2 days, depending on how busy and popular your exchange is.

- Choosing a deposit method: Different exchanges have different banking methods. You could find a mixture of PayPal or credit/debit card payments, SEPA, or bank wire transfers and different methods attract different charges. You can find details of charges in the footer of the website of the exchange, before making any deposit.

- Making a deposit: This can be done using your fiat currency like Euros, US dollars, etc. The time taken for deposits to reflect in your exchange account may range from a few hours to several days, depending on the deposit method and the exchange you used.

- Finally, you can start buying Ether using the funds that you have deposited: Different exchanges have interfaces that work differently, but you should be ready to go through verification procedures and then pause for a while to allow the system to process your transaction. Processing time varies depending on the total number of transactions requested at a time. You'll find it easy to perform this step on Coinbase because it's more user friendly than other platforms. Good luck!

Sometimes, buying Ethereum may appear to be such a long process since the traditional banking system is very slow. Bank and credit card payments require laborious verification processes and most exchanges will always have to wait for clearance of payments before availing Ether to you. However, remember these are online transactions and you can risk losing your investment. Therefore, the following activities can form part of your due diligence process.

- Always copy and paste your wallet address: Avoid typing the wallet address by hand. Remember, a wallet address is long and case-sensitive, meaning you will lose your funds forever if you make any single mistake. This is because Ethereum does not have charge back or customer support number that you can instantly call to get help.

- Checking the transaction fee: Normally, the system will show you the calculated fee in your local fiat currency, say in dollars and cents. Don't just hurry. Take time and confirm whether the transaction fee is reasonable or not.

- Confirming the address at least 3 times: After copying and pasting the address which you would like to receive or send Ether to, ascertain that it is correct by checking it over and over. The easiest way to do this is by scrutinizing the first and last digits or letters to make sure that they are pasted correctly. This is an important step, even though a good Ethereum wallet software would still confirm the address that you would like to send or receive Ether to.

- Testing your transaction: As you begin, try to send an insignificant amount of Ether in order to confirm that all the details are correct, and also test your overall understanding of the process. By so doing, you will gain confidence and perform transactions that involve sending larger amounts smoothly. You don't have to worry about cost since Ethereum's adoption is hinged on low transaction fees.

- Also, as noted earlier on, learn how to secure your Ethereum wallet. You may store your Ether in your wallet or leave it on the exchange. However, this exposes you to a greater level of risk since you may not be able to audit and ensure the security of your exchange. There may be cases of digital theft or platform failure. Therefore, you shouldn't go for this option.

If the funds you're storing are relatively small compared to your overall portfolio, then you can secure your Ether on your Exchange. However, such a move means that you will not own your private key and the Exchange assumes the responsibility of your Ether. Given the fact that exchanges don't operate the way banks do, i.e. traditional financial regulations aren't applicable to exchanges, any theft or insolvency means that you automatically lose your funds.

Depending on the method you use to secure your Ether, below are a few tips that you can adopt:

- 2 Factor Authentication (2FA): This is another security process in which you will be required to input a one-time password (OTP) before you can login to your wallet, or perform any transaction. Most Ethereum wallets rely on the Google Authenticator app for 2FA. Also, different exchanges and wallets implement 2FA in different ways; even though additional security feature provided remains the same. With a 2FA, a potential thief must have your password and obtain access to the physical device from which to generate the OTP. Using a 2FA app, such as Google Authenticator, has had good ratings amongst many internet users.

  However, some wallets or exchanges may opt to avoid the use of an app and just send an OTP in the form of an SMS. Avoid SMS 2FA since the OTP can easily be seen even if the phone remains unlocked. And the worst-case scenario is that with social engineering, telecoms staff have been convinced to port a phone number to any new SIM. This implies that the phone number alone can be instrumental in accessing any platform that is purportedly secured by SMS 2FA.

- Using multi-signature wallets: Such wallets potentially secure your Ethereum by ensuring that multiple participants have to sign each and every transaction you undertake. A typical multi signature wallet is rated as "2 of 3," which means that at least 2 out of the total 3 private keys have to sign the transaction to enable successful broadcasting to the Ethereum network. In such a case, you may consider splitting the 3 private keys over diverse physical locations as well as their own physical security to make sure that not even a single point of attack takes place. All in all, different wallets implement multi-signature wallets in different ways. So always find out what options they have and integrate them in your plans.

With extra security layers, it's important to assess your level of risk tolerance before settling on your preferred security option. Please keep in mind that cryptoasset security practices keep evolving each and every day, so it is a good idea to consult your wallet or exchange and get their recommendations in order to avoid any security pitfalls that may affect your novel investment measures.

With time, you may find that you are not interested in buying Ethereum anymore, but would just like to speculate on its price. In such cases, you can try day trading and creatively discover how to maximize your profits.

Day Trading Ethereum

Apart from buying and selling Ether tokens, another form of trading Ethereum is through CFD trading. CFD, commonly known as a Contract For Difference, is a stock market term that involves arrangements made in a futures contract that allows for differences in settlement to be made through payment of cash, instead of the delivery of physical securities and or goods/services. Futures in this case refer to a unique kind of investment asset that you can use to invest in diverse commodities. Futures are known to determine global prices for essential commodities, like oil, while supporting complex markets, like those markets meant for agricultural products.

By purchasing an Ethereum future, it means that you are essentially signing a contract that will enable you to buy something at a given date in the future, and at a specific price. For instance, suppose you choose to buy an Ethereum future worth 1,000 Ethereum token, then you are essentially buying a contract that can allow for the delivery of 1,000 Ethereum token, when the contract becomes due. With experience, you'll even sell your futures contract before it is due and get the tokens delivered to you.

On the other hand, you can choose to avoid getting the commodity, say Ethereum, physically delivered by purchasing a contract for difference. In this case, you'll reach an agreement with your seller on how cash payments on any differences in the rise and fall of prices will be made without the delivery of the physical goods. Therefore, CFD trading will enable you to take risks with the rising or falling prices of fast-moving international financial markets or instruments, such as treasuries, currencies, commodities, indices, and shares.

With Ethereum CFD trading, you can still tap into the benefits and risks of trading with Ethereum tokens, without buying or selling the physical Ethereum tokens. All you need to do is to purchase a contract that entitles you to the value of the Ethereum that you would have bought, and essentially you end up buying and selling Ethereum tokens even though you don't actually own the cryptocurrency itself.

For example, maybe you are quite certain that the price of Ethereum is bound to increase in a few days' time and choose to invest in it. Therefore, you can purchase the contract for difference in which you and the seller of the contract can reach an agreement to settle any drop or rise in prices in cash when the contract ends (preferably referred to as the contract date). In simple terms, you can sign a CFD with a busy company like Plus500 for Ether at today's value, and set the contract to end at 10pm (probably due to the fact that Plus500's Ethereum trades must end by 10pm). Thus, the value to be traded will be set by the current price of Ethereum.

In the meantime, you will have to set a definite time for your contract, say the forthcoming several hours, which defines the point at which either the buyer (you) or the seller gets to be paid any difference occurring in prices. At the end of the day, should your intuition about variation in Ethereum prices turn out to be correct, and prices vary within that time frame, the trading company, in this case Plus500, will pay you the difference. However, if your intuition ends up being incorrect with prices not going as you had projected, then you will be forced to pay the difference to the trading company.

This form of trading can be likened to "gambling" on the value of the Ethereum token since both the seller and buyer bet on whether or not Ethereum prices are likely to rise or drop, although the whole process is more complex than it appears. It is important to note that Ethereum CFD trading puts your capital at risk. Therefore, you need some prior experience in trading with Ethereum, especially in terms of understanding the market volatility, in order to reap big with this form of trading.

CFD trading has such benefits as:

- You don't have to hold real Ethereum tokens: This means that you don't waste time trying to secure the Ethereum tokens that you would have purchased. Also, you eventually eliminate the risk of losing your Ethereum tokens.

- You can benefit from liquidity that is provided by other trading institutions: With CFD trading, individuals don't have to trade with each other over a given exchange. However, on a CFD platform, you'll be guaranteed full access to liquidity from institutional partners and this makes the Ethereum transactions as instant as you would like them to be.

- Lower taxes: Sometimes, depending on your jurisdiction, you may incur lower tax rates on profits earned from Ethereum CFD trading than when you just buy and sell Ethereum directly.

- Shorting the market: Even though some exchanges may allow you to short the market, it is far much easier to set up a short position when you are doing Ethereum CFD trading.

While Ethereum CFD trading will accord you some level of convenience and flexibility, it doesn't just take place without some challenges. Some of these challenges are:

- Spreads: As you start going long or short on Ethereum, you are likely to suffer some losses of the spread. This essentially refers to the difference between the price at which you buy (commonly known as asking price) and the price at which you sell (commonly referred to as bidding price). The loss can range from as low as 0.5% to as high as 5% of the total amount traded. At times, you may be charged a commission over and above the spread, thereby grossly affecting your earnings.

- Fees: Most Ethereum CFD trading platforms normally have a certain fee on trades that may have been left open overnight. This can become very costly, especially if your trades roll over for days. Therefore, if you are on short term day trading,; always ask for incentives from your Ethereum CFD trading platform so that you can be covered against the higher risk.

Other forms of Ethereum trading include:

- Binary trading: This is another form of Ethereum trading though it involves a high level of risk. It is not recommended for beginners because it involves price prediction that takes place within a very short period of time, which is typically after every few minutes. As such, binary trading heavily relies on luck and winning on it may become extremely difficult, in the long run. Therefore, Ethereum binary trading is considered to be a form of gambling and used mainly for entertainment purposes, just like when people enjoy the spin of a roulette wheel while reveling. Binary trading is not a better way if you want to do serious Ethereum trading. However, if you would like to try it out, you can implement the following platform-independent strategies to help you reduce the risks of fixed losses:

  o Martingale system: This is one of the oldest strategies that has grown in popularity among investors in cryptocurrency. To implement this strategy, you need to establish an initial stake and position. If your binary option turns out to be successful, then you have to continue with the same stake. However, if your binary option fails, then you have to double the stake for the next position. The motivation factor and main idea behind this strategy lies in the fact that you will eventually make a successful binary trade option, as time passes by. Thus, even if you fail to succeed in your past binary options, you are likely to neutralize your losses by eventually making significant gains in profits.

o D'Alembert system: This strategy builds on the concept of Martingale system, but systematically modifies it. With D'Alembert system, you have to increase your investment after a loss but decrease it after a win. For instance, if 1 unit is your initial stake, then a loss essentially means that your next stake must be 2 units. If you lose further, then you will have to increase the subsequent stake to 3 units, a process that continues until you register a win. Now, if you win, you will have to decrease the stake by a single unit. E.g. if you started with 4 units, then the next will be made of 3 units, and this continues up to when you reach your goal.

These strategies appear to be very exciting, but must be implemented with a lot of caution. You don't want to be left gasping for breath when the reality of making huge unexpected losses dawns on you. But if you have developed a thick skin and can withstand abrupt losses, then these strategies can help you generate stable revenues and splendid profit margins that can keep you smiling all the way. As a rule of thumb, always avoid risking large sums of Ether.

- Ethereum margin trading: Would you like to purchase larger volumes of Ether but you have limited capital? Would you like to try leveraging on other people's capital? Then Ethereum margin trading is what you can opt for. As a margin trader, you will be provided with access to borrowing so that you can purchase any volume of Ether that you would like to. Normally, the initial margin, which basically refers to the amount that you can borrow, varies in size and is determined by the brokerage. Just like many other traders, you are likely to discover that buying Ethereum on margin is extremely profitable. Ethereum margin trading has a few risks as well, but performing your market research processes well will help you mitigate against these risks. Still, margin accounts are normally capped with a "maintenance requirement" in order to stop traders from undertaking excessive borrowing. The maintenance requirement just stipulates the least amount that you must have in equity on your account before you can be allowed to undertake further borrowing.

For instance, suppose you deposit $5,000 and move ahead to borrow $5,000 more in order to buy Ether worth *$10,000, AND THIS PROMPTS YOUR BROKERAGE TO SET THE MAINTENANCE REQUIREMENT ON YOUR MARGIN ACCOUNT AT 25%. THEN IF THE VALUE OF THE ETHER THAT YOU PURCHASED FALLS TO* $8,000, you will be required to have not less than $2,000 (25% of $8,000) in equity. Incidentally, your total equity value is $3,000 ($5,000 – $2,000). However, suppose the price of Ether drops further such that your total equity value falls to less than $3,000, then your brokerage will have to issue a "margin call" and dispose of your Ether in order to return your account to its maintenance requirement.

Ethereum investment can be quite involving at times. However, the hustle is worth it, considering the fact that any effective single move can significantly increase your earnings. Therefore, always be on the watch out. Continue engaging your exchange in order to keep scouting for emerging amazing investment opportunities. The more you engage with your exchange, the more you will discover potential deals, coupons, promotions and offers that could make a great difference in your investment portfolio.

Sometimes, your exchange may not allow you to store funds in your local fiat currency. And if that is possible, you may have to jump through a few hoops in order to lock in your profits. The normal procedure is that you have to sell your Ether tokens and transfer the money back to your account before locking in profits. This means that you must send the money back to the exchange to make subsequent Ether purchases, a flurry of activities that can be tedious and time consuming. However, by using Tether, these processes can become more manageable. Tether is not a cryptocurrency. It is attached to the US dollar, with one Tether being worth approximately $1 USD.

By trading your Ether for USDT, you can easily lock in your profits. Likewise, whenever you want to buy Ether again, just trade your USDT back on the exchange. By so doing, you will minimize the extended waiting times, especially if you're a regular trader.

Perhaps you are not interested in buying or earning Ethereum. This shouldn't hinder you from trading with Ethereum, because you could still make use of Ethereum mining and keep increasing the amount of your Ethereum tokens. Therefore, in the next chapter, we are going to explore Ethereum mining.

Chapter 3: Ethereum Mining

To begin with, the Ethereum network boasts of providing a platform for developing several applications that can promote sustainable development in all spheres of life while helping organizations maximize profits.

Essentially, Ethereum mining is the process that makes Ether available for traders, so that the Ethereum network can continue running. Let's attempt to define Ethereum mining.

What's Ethereum Mining?

Mining simply refers to a computational intensive work that utilizes a lot of time and power. Mining gives room for peer participation in a distributed cryptocurrency network, on the basis of consensus. The mining process makes use of the computer's hardware as well as mining applications, and results in rewarding the miner for providing solutions to complex math problems.

It's important to note that all transactions in Ethereum are embedded within separate data blocks, which are comparable to those transaction batches that banks send to each other, even though Ethereum ones occur in intervals of 15 seconds. Also, blocks are distinguished by their "height," which starts from zero and increases sequentially up to the current block, and each block has internal links to several other blocks resulting to a blockchain. Once these blocks are formed, they need prompt analysis in order to guarantee a smooth running of transactions on the platform.

However, in practice, most issuers of Ether may lack the processing abilities to do this alone. Therefore, this creates an opportunity for miners. As such, a miner refers to any investor devoting their energy, computer space, and time in order to examine the blocks. Once the mining process hits the correct harsh, miners subsequently submit the accrued solutions to the issuer for verification purposes. Then, the issuer of the cryptocurrency rewards the miners with digital coins in exchange for the miners' work, and further offers portions of the verified transactions as rewards. Digital mining results in proof of work system. Some currencies rely on this system alone while others make use of a combination of proof of work and proof of stake.

Please note that the word *mining* stems from the gold resemblance of the sphere of cryptocurrency. This means that it doesn't operate like some sort of get rich quick schemes, but demands heavy inputs in terms of time, equipment and effort in order to grow, especially when working single-handedly. The word *mining* is widely used in that just as it is rare to find precious materials, so is the case with digital currencies. Briefly, Ethereum mining refers to the process of mining Ether and it involves securing the network in order to guarantee verified computation.

Remember, the smooth running of the Ethereum network relies on Ether. Simply put, Ether is actually the incentive used to encourage developers to come up with top notch applications. And as a developer who wishes to engage and use smart contracts on the Ethereum network, you must have Ether in order to proceed. Thus, Ether acts as the fuel for the Ethereum network and mining is normally considered as the cheapest way of running transactions on the Ethereum network when compared to just buying Ether.

Always keep in mind that Ether is not all that infinite. This is because Ether's overall amount as well as its network operations was set during the 2014 presale, meaning, the number of Ether issued within a single year should not exceed 18 million, which is essentially 25% of the initial issue. This measure was taken in order for it to act as a system that checks on inflation.

For a block to be validated in consensus, proof of work for the specific difficulty must be provided. Esthash, a *memory-hard* algorithm that's meant to counter the development of Ethereum-mining, is the algorithm used for validation and it operates by identifying the nonce input (an arbitrary number that can only be used once) to the result in such a manner that it falls below the threshold that the difficulty determines. If the end results are identical in distribution, then the fact that the duration of time taken to find a nonce is based on the difficulty is most assured. Therefore, a miner can control the time required to find a new block by just manipulating the difficulty. In Ethereum mining, the difficulty is modified dynamically to enable the network release a single block after an interval of 12 seconds on average. The system then undertakes such rapid synchronization that it becomes impossible to rewrite history or maintain a fork, unless if the individual trying to do so can control more than half of the network's mining power.

In a nutshell, the process of Ethereum mining entails:

- A miner taking note of transactions on the Ethereum network and amassing everything that's deemed valid (e.g. code, fees, as well as the accounting history of who is in charge of the individual coins) into various blocks.

- A miner consuming electricity to *hash* that block using the GPU's processing power. With each successful hash result, a unique proof of work is produced in order to prove that the miner worked on the given block. *A hash refers to a mathematical procedure that takes a variable amount of data and leads to the production of a shorter, fixed-length output.*

- If the hashed block is accepted by the entire Ethereum network as valid, then the block is automatically incorporated into the blockchain, as part of the lasting consensus on valid transactions.

- Finally, the miner gets 5 ETH on top of all code-processing and transaction fees (or gas) available in their block, as well as possible bonuses for any uncles (other blockchains that are not part of the initial parent blockchain) that may have been involved.

The process of Ethereum mining may appear complex and quite involving, but this should not scare you. Many applications have been developed to make it as simple as possible. Before delving into the details of these applications, let's explore some of the reasons as to why you may prefer to undertake Ethereum mining.

The Importance of Ethereum Mining

You can benefit from Ethereum mining in such ways as:

- Ethereum mining is the surest way to gain voice and support the Ethereum network, especially if you are interested in the concept of Ethereum.

- By mining Ethereum, you will build a large ETH position in this proof of work phase, and you'll earn interest on your holdings if/when Ethereum moves to a proof of stake phase.

- Mining gives you the cheapest entry ticket to the Ethereum markets. As such, given the prevailing volatility of Ethereum markets and as a good trader, you can simply maximize your profits.

- Since Ethereum is easily traded for Bitcoins, you can gradually and cheaply build your Bitcoin holding position by mining Ethereum.

- Bitcoins are easily traded for cash. Therefore, through Ethereum mining, you can indirectly earn cash or even fill up your bank account. You can directly sell your Ether on a number of leading exchanges (like Coinbase, Gemini, Kraken, BTC-e, Bitfinex, etc.) and earn cash.

- You can also subsidize the purchase of a new, top-of-the-line GPU through Ethereum mining.

So, isn't it a great idea to mine Ethereum, instead of buying Ether? Certainly, based on the above benefits, Ethereum mining is one of the best ways to learn and evolve with the Ethereum technology. You can do Ethereum mining in the comfort of your home, as long as you possess some knowledge of the command prompt and a flair for script writing. This section outlines a few steps that can get you started with Ethereum mining. With persistent practice, you will realize that Ethereum mining is quite easy, exciting and tremendously fulfilling.

But before we dive into Ethereum mining, let's look at some of the basics that you need to pay extra attention to:

- Always keep in mind that Ethereum mining consumes a lot of electricity. This means that you have to manage your mining practices in a way that is so efficient that you can generate more income through the sale of Ether. The good news is that there is no need to get worked up because you'll eventually get some profits. Therefore, use mining calculators to determine your profits and avoid making unnecessary losses. We will explore Ethereum mining profitability calculator later on.

For power supply, always double-check that there are sufficient connections on the PSU in order to support all the GPUs that you're running. Your overall wattage should also be enough in order to support your total system power draw; don't forget to give yourself a 10-15% buffer. You can refer here: http://www.realhardtechx.com/index.html for guidance on the number of 6 or 8 pin PCI-E power connections that your GPU requires. You may also use an online power consumption calculator to determine your overall system power draw.

Besides, if you want to build multiple rigs, then you can consider sticking with the same brand PSU so that you can use the additional cables on other systems when deemed fit. For instance, suppose you decide to use EVGA G2 PSU's only, and you end up having extra molex, sata or VGA cables from one build, then just go ahead and use them on another build.

Please get a simple PC power button switch, which can connect onto the motherboard headers so that you can easily turn your system on/off.

- Ethereum mining can be done on any personal computer, as long as the system has a GPU (Graphic Card) with a RAM rating of at least 2GB. Don't do Ethereum mining on a Central Processing Unit (CPU) because such would be an exercise in futility. If you choose to mine Ethereum on a CPU, the exercise will take a prolonged period of time to complete and your profits will be very little. But GPUs are 200 times faster than CPUs. Besides, Ethereum is also designed to function well on a memory hard hashing technique, which a GPU is good at it. Always go for AMD cards, since they're more efficient than Nvidia cards.

- Also, ensure that your computer system's hard drive has a lot of free space. Please note that the blockchain and other software require a hardware memory space of approximately 30GB. Your gaming laptop may have a high-end card. But given the high amount of heat generated from mining, your laptop may be damaged, as a result. Therefore, always use a desktop build. Also, avoid using rented virtualized environments because they may lack sufficient GPU or they may not be that profitable. Your system should also meet the following minimum requirements:

  o Must have a 64-bit installation Windows 10 OS. This is because you can easily configure Windows and get it running as fast as possible.

    Just go to "Start Menu > Services" and set setup to automatic in order to activate the Windows Time service because this service may be disabled by default, especially in Windows 10.

o   The motherboard must have enough PCI-E slots in order to sustain all the cards that you are running.

o   When using more than 1 GPU, please provide each additional GPU with a powered pci-e riser.

o   Buy a simple low-end CPU with RAM of at least 4GB. Your RAM, CPU, and motherboard should be compatible as well. That is, 1151 socket CPU goes with LGA 1151 motherboards, while LGA 1150 motherboards/DDR4 RAM takes a DDR3 RAM and 1150 CPU.

o   A standard monitor, mouse and keyboard are also necessary. At an advanced level, where you manage your rig remotely, getting a headless HDMI dummy plug that you will plug into your rig and enable proper booting into Windows for remote access, is also a good idea.

Finally, don't use ASICs for Ethereum mining, although ASICs are profitable for mining other coins, like Litecoin, Dash and Bitcoin.

Armed with the above tips, now is the time to put your best foot forward. Now it's the time to do Ethereum mining!

The Ethereum Mining Procedure

You can mine Ethereum by following the steps below:

1. Download the Geth application, which will act as a communication hub, meant to coordinate your setup and report emerging developments that would require your attention as well as linking you to the Ethereum platform. This means that whenever a block is mined by another computer, your Geth application automatically picks it and relays the new information onto your GPU for mining.

2. Geth is a zip file. Therefore, unzip and transfer it to the hard drive. You can move it to drive C, so that the subsequent steps can be easier to follow. Copy the file you just downloaded and unzipped, then have it moved to the hard drive folder.

3. To execute the installed application, you must run the Command Prompt. Therefore, while in the Windows search function, search for 'CMD,' and click on it from the list of the search results.

4. The Command Prompt should be opened by now. It may look terrifying, especially if you're new to it. The command prompt box is normally displayed as 'C:\Users\Username>.' Username is your username; if you log into your computer using cryptocompare as your username, then your Command Prompt box will be opened as C:\Users\cryptocompare>. At this point, you've to ask the computer to look elsewhere in order to locate Geth. Type 'cd/' into the command prompt terminal, in which case you're issuing an instruction to "change directory". Thishighlights 'C:\>' essentially showing that you are in C: drive.

5. You can now create a new account. Making a call to Geth is simple. Just type in 'geth account new' then press the enter key. This will enable the command terminal to show 'C:\>geth account new.'

6. You'll be required to create a password. Here, you need to be very careful, because you won't be able to see what you're typing. Remember, this password essentially locks your account and ensures that your Private Key is safe, so losing this password means that you'll also lose all the Ether that's attached to your wallet that's held by your Private Key, so you must be sure about your password. You may have to write it down before typing it carefully into the machine. Once you finish typing your password, press enter. This automatically creates your new account.

7. At this juncture, let Geth link up with the Ethereum network in order to become fully operational. So type "geth --rpc" in the terminal before pressing enter, to initiate the download of Ethereum's blockchain and synchronize with the entire global network. This is a time intensive process that largely relies on your internet's connection speed the current size of the blockchain. Therefore, be patient and wait for this process to end before you can start mining. If your firewall tries to block this process, remember to click "allow access." Let this cmd remain open; it must run in the background as you mine. You may also be asked to specify whether you're interested in mining on the hard fork chain or not. So, to mine Ether, just use "geth --rpc --support-dao-fork."

8. Before moving further, get a mining software. A mining software will help your GPU to run the hash the Ethereum platform's algorithm. You can go for Ethminer, download then install Ethminer. Look for the latest version download it and install.

Again, if firewall prevents the process, just click "allow" and if Windows can't recognize it, click "ok" as well.

9. Then, open up a new command terminal, as in step 4 above, and get 2 terrifying boxes. You need to modify directory command. Just right-click on the terminal icon, the one that has been active, found in the task bar at the bottom of the page, before clicking on the on-command prompt in the resultant menu.

10. Then type "cd /" in the command prompt that has just been opened to give "C:\users\username>cd /" and press the enter key. Now, "C:\>" should be on display. This means that you have used the "change directory" ("cd") command cause command prompt look at C:/ drive, and not your user file.

11. Next, press the tab button after typing in "cd prog." This will look this way: C:\>cd prog. Press "tab" to automatically wind up the phrase for the closest fit that's available in the C: drive, the same way autotext behaves on your Iphone. Once you press "tab," this, C:/> cd "Program Files," should appear. Then press enter to bring forth a new line that says, "C:\Program Files>."

12. You can access the Ethereum Mining software that you've just installed by simply typing in cd cpp before pressing the tab key. Then press enter. After pressing tab, you'll find C:\Program Files>cd cpp-ethereum; after pressing enter you'll get C:\Program Files\cpp-ethereum>.

13. And voila! Now you can start mining Ethereum. Key in 'ethminer –G' before pressing the enter key. This automatically initiates the mining process after building the Directed Acyclic Graph (DAG), a large file that is stored in your GPU's RAM in order to make it Application Specific Integrated Circuits (ASIC) resistant. This step requires enough space on your hard drive, so ensure you meet

the basics of mining as stated above.

14. Whenever you get error messages, you can cancel the process by pressing Ctrl and C. Then retry the process to get a successful attempt.

15. You can also perform CPU mining. Type in 'ETHMINER' before pressing the enter key for the process to begin. DAG will still be built before Geth begins to communicate with Ethminer.

16. Since the hashrate of the network continues to climb, solo mining is becoming more difficult. Therefore, for good profits feel free to join a **mining pool** and learn from the best-established industry practices.

Should the above process of Ethereum mining prove difficult, you can try cloud mining. Cloud mining is relatively easy, even though not as profitable.

Ethereum Cloud Mining

If you're not tech savvy or can't just devote enough time to Ethereum mining, then cloud mining is a viable option that you can consider as well. Cloud mining simply refers to a business concept that enables you to buy a share of the mining hardware that's located in remote data centers.

With cloud mining, you will have to pay another person to mine for you and even manage and operate the mining system on your behalf. You'll be required to enter into a one-year contract, where you pay the mining company upfront and let them do the work for you. You get an opportunity to get a little revenue and some frequent payouts at a low level of risk. Maintenance and electricity costs no longer concern you in cloud mining.

There are a number of reputable firms that offer cloud mining. However, always be careful or you risk losing your investment. Genesis is one such company from which you can get your first mining contract and start earning with no hassle. You're likely to get better deals in Ethereum cloud mining due to:

- Cloud miners buy in bulk and end up getting discounts on the purchase of their GPUs.

- Cloud miners mostly put their machines in low cost locations.

These measures significantly reduce the operation costs for running Ethereum mining machines, and the savings are subsequently passed on to you. For instance, Genesis mining contracts are run off green energy, which considerably reduces mining expenses.

Another advantage of using cloud miners is that they guarantee 100% uptime. As such, they're ready to substitute their own machines whenever your miner goes offline. Finally, by using cloud miners, you won't have to listen to the noise that results from the mining process.

Other companies that offer cloud mining are:

- Crypterra: This is a new company that offers a 2-year contract of ETH cloud mining.

- Hashflare: At Hashflare, there are no fixed contracts or hidden fees, but you get instant withdrawals once you sign a contract with them.

You can start cloud mining by simply buying shares online and joining a cloud mining pool. Just select your preferred plan, make the necessary payments and start mining. Even though Ethereum market may be considered transparent, you must be awake as scamming companies may be on the prowl to swindle your hard-earned cash.

All in all, mining requires a lot of practice. Even with no background in IT related fields, you can still earn more from mining. This guide hasn't covered the more advanced steps of mining, like Dual mining, remote access and monitoring, bios flashing, overlocking and undervolting. However, you can advance your skills in these areas by enrolling for mining classes.

Having a reliable system that keeps track of your performance can keep you motivated as you go on with Ethereum mining. You can also measure the success of your mining system by monitoring the profits you make. Next, let's see how to do this.

Ethereum Mining Profitability Calculator

Mining is a resource intensive exercise, which can easily drain your investments if not undertaken with a lot of care. For this reason, many tools have been developed to enhance the effectiveness of your system. These tools are profitability calculators that forecast the net hash as well as the daily Ether, and can help you determine whether the exercise is worthwhile. Below are some steps that you can follow to determine the profitability of your system:

- Before embarking on Ethereum mining, it is a good idea to have a look at Etherscan's Mining Calculator to be updated on such issues as the network hashrate (which represents billions of calculations within a second and are normally measured in Gigahash per second (GH/s), block time and current Ether prices.)

- Once, you've obtained the above figures, copy them into the Cryptowizzard Mining Calculator, which is an advanced calculator and enables you to set your electricity costs. Remember, electricity costs play a very critical role in determining your mining profits.

- Next, you can select the Graphics card that you wish to use. This will prompt the calculator to automatically enter the correct power consumption and hashrate. Suppose you've modified your card's performance or your card isn't listed, then just select the Custom option and perform a manual entry of the appropriate figures. Remember to enter GPU hashrates in MH/s (Megahash per second), which denotes millions of calculations within a second.

- Now you can enter the price of your electricity. This information can be obtained from **here** or **here** if you are in the US or elsewhere respectively, or by just referring to your utility bill. After entering all the figures correctly, you should see the profits that you're bound to generate.

These figures vary from time to time. From the above example, you notice that the miner would net 109 ETH per year. Suppose the Ether is sold at the current price, then the miner will earn $1537. So, after subtracting the electricity cost of $493, the miner's net profit amounts to $1045. The miner may deduct several other deductions such as:

- 1% plus a 1 ETH payout fee as pool mining costs.

- The purchase price of system components.

- Buying a new power supply unit (PSU); it's most recommended that you purchase an electricity efficient PSU. Even though it may cost you more, you'll inevitably save on power cost.

However, please keep in mind that the future of Ethereum remains unpredictable for most actors. Mining difficulty is still on the rising trend and it may even spike as many more efficient GPUs are released. Further, the scheduled switch of Ethereum from the current proof of work model to proof of stake model at an unspecified date means that it will no longer be possible to mine Ethereuem. Therefore, be prepared to cope with the tough times, when your profits begin dwindling.

Any investor knows that change is inevitable. As you begin to invest in Ethereum, it is important to be prepared for any eventuality, since such could have far-reaching ramifications on your earnings. The next chapter delves into the future of Ethereum so that you can understand the market better and make more informed plans to handle forthcoming challenges.

Chapter 4: The Future of Ethereum

Experts argue that Ethereum network is expected to expand and grow into a unique platform that can offer solutions to day-to-day problems. Therefore, it's a good idea to keep abreast of the upcoming changes that will happen to Ethereum network and devise innovative ways to keep your online investment safe.

First and foremost, the process of launching Ethereum was divided into 4 phases. This was necessitated by the need to ensure that all the phases had ample developmental time in order to ensure efficient and optimal development. The 4 phases of Ethereum launch are:

- Frontier phase: This was the first phase. It was largely described as an experimental phase. During this phase, Ethereum underwent several strategic protocol upgrades to enhance its functionality and incentive structures.

- Homestead phase: This is the current phase, which is considered to be stable, and has experienced improvements to security, gas pricing, and transaction pricing.

- Metropolis phase: This is the upcoming phase and is aimed at reducing the complexity of the EVM as well as providing a bit of flexibility for smart contracts.

- Serenity phase: This is the final stage. Even though the move to Serenity is uncertain, this phase is meant to be characterized by an essential shift from proof-of-work (hardware mining) to proof-of-stake (virtual mining).

Please note that the Ethereum network is expected to switch to the Metropolis phase, any time from now. With such a move, the following concepts will be evident:

- Abstraction: This implies that you can just use any protocol or system even if you completely don't know the ins and outs as well as all the technical details. For instance, you don't need to be an engineer or a programmer to operate your iPhone. Thus, you can activate an app by simply pressing on the screen, or you can call someone by just pressing the call button. Simply put, abstraction removes the complexities and makes a complex technology accessible to the masses.

   In other words, abstraction will allow you to use any cryptocurrency, like Bitcoin, to pay for Ethereum transactions.

- Zk-Snarks: This is an acronym for "Zero-Knowledge Succinct Non-interactive Argument of Knowledge." It operates on the concept of zero knowledge proofs. For example, suppose we have two parties, like the prover and the verifier, the prover may ascertain that they're party to the given information to the verifier, even though the information itself isn't revealed. Consequently, introduction of Zk-Snarks on Ethereum will enhance privacy and make online trading more comfortable to masses.

- Sharding: In this case, a huge database, like a blockchain, is broken down into parts that are smaller and more manageable. These parts are commonly referred to as "shards." As such, individual shards must have their own sets of validators. Therefore, proof-of-stakes is an essential requirement for this to occur. Now, in the current proof-of-work phase, all miners work on the same problem simultaneously. But sharding separates validators into designated shards, thereby ensuring that they can all work on different problems at the same time. Meaning, the efficiency of the whole system is enhanced, because of the implementation of the Ethereum Improvement Protocols (EIPs). Therefore, Ethereum contracts will be more flexible and start paying their own fees even without external funding from users.

And so, the switch to the Metropolis will see the implementation of the long-awaited move from the proof-of-work model to the proof-of-stakes model. The proof-of-work model involves using dedicated hardware to solve crypto-puzzles in order to mine Ehtereum. But the proof-of-stakes model is bound to make the whole mining process more virtual, by using validators instead of miners.

Therefore, if you're interested in mining, you should be prepared to become a validator once the switch occurs. As a validator, you will be required to lock up some of your Ether as stake, before being allowed to validate blocks. Validation work will be simple. You will just scout for those blocks that you feel can be appended to the blockchain and place bets on them. So, if your block gets appended, you'll be rewarded and your reward will be proportional to the stake you invested. However, you'll lose your stake by placing a bet on the wrong block.

Casper consensus algorithm will be used to implement the proof-of-stake model. The initial stages will see a hybrid style system that will allow a majority of transactions on proof-of-work model while every 100th transaction will be done on the proof-of-stake model. So, you don't need to worry because you'll have an opportunity to test your skills on the new model before it is fully implemented.

All in all, the future of Ethereum looks bright because the main objective of the Ethereum network is to become ubiquitous. And in the same breath, the success of Ethereum will be determined by the perception of the public towards the tokens launched on the platform, decisions made by the development team and the quality of the apps launched on the platform. Thus, Ethereum will run everything and you won't even have an idea that you're working on something that relies on it. However, a lot of work still needs to be done in order to achieve that, so investing in Ethereum now isn't a bad idea. As you invest, always keep in mind that you're trading in a very immature market, and anything can happen at any time. Despite the fact that there's great potential in its technology, try to limit your risk since the market is bound to experience a lot of volatility. Good luck!

Conclusion

Investing in Ethereum is one of the ways you can use to hedge against economic uncertainty, just like possessing gold. With Ether transactions gaining traction globally, you need not to wait any longer before letting your investment count.

If you found the book valuable, can you recommend it to others? One way to do that is to post a review on Amazon.